I0801562

AMERICAN ★ HISTORY

The INDUSTRIAL REVOLUTION

The Birth of Modern America

By Emily Mahoney

Portions of this book originally appeared in *The Industrial Revolution* by Kevin Hillstrom.

LUCENT PRESS

Published in 2018 by
Lucent Press, an Imprint of Greenhaven Publishing, LLC
353 3rd Avenue
Suite 255
New York, NY 10010

Copyright © 2018 Greenhaven Press, a part of Gale, Cengage Learning
Gale and Greenhaven Press are registered trademarks used herein under license.

All new materials copyright © 2018 Lucent Press, an Imprint of Greenhaven Publishing, LLC.

All rights reserved. No part of this book may be reproduced in any form without permission in writing from the publisher, except by a reviewer.

Designer: Deanna Paternostro
Editor: Siyavush Saidian

Library of Congress Cataloging-in-Publication Data

Names: Mahoney, Emily.
Title: The Industrial Revolution: the birth of modern America / Emily Mahoney.
Description: New York : Lucent Press, 2018. | Series: American history | Includes index.
Identifiers: ISBN 9781534561335 (library bound) | ISBN 9781534561342 (ebook)
Subjects: LCSH: Industrial revolution–United States–Juvenile literature. | Industries–United States–History–Juvenile literature. | Technological innovations–Social aspects–United States–History–Juvenile literature. | United States–Economic conditions–Juvenile literature.
Classification: LCC HC105.M22 2018 | DDC 330.973'08–dc23

Printed in the United States of America

CPSIA compliance information: Batch #BS17KL: For further information contact Greenhaven Publishing LLC, New York, New York at 1-844-317-7404.

Please visit our website, www.greenhavenpublishing.com. For a free color catalog of all our high-quality books, call toll free 1-844-317-7404 or fax 1-844-317-7405.

Contents

Foreword

The United States is a relatively young country. It has existed as its own nation for more than 200 years, but compared to nations such as China that have existed since ancient times, it is still in its infancy. However, the United States has grown and accomplished much since its birth in 1776. What started as a loose confederation of former British colonies has grown into a major world power whose influence is felt around the globe.

How did the United States manage to develop into a global superpower in such a short time? The answer lies in a close study of its unique history. The story of America is unlike any other—filled with colorful characters, a variety of exciting settings, and events too incredible to be anything other than true.

Too often, the experience of history is lost among the basic facts: names, dates, places, laws, treaties, and battles. These fill countless textbooks, but they are rarely compelling on their own. Far more interesting are the stories that surround those

basic facts. It is in discovering those stories that students are able to see history as a subject filled with life—and a subject that says as much about the present as it does about the past.

The titles in this series allow readers to immerse themselves in the action at pivotal historical moments. They also encourage readers to discuss complex issues in American history—many of which still affect Americans today. These include racism, states' rights, civil liberties, and many other topics that are in the news today but have their roots in the earliest days of America. As such, readers are encouraged to think critically about history and current events.

Each title is filled with excellent tools for research and analysis. Fully cited quotations from historical figures, letters, speeches, and documents provide students with firsthand accounts of major events. Primary sources bring authority to the text, as well. Sidebars highlight these quotes and primary sources, as well as interesting figures and events. Annotated bibliographies allow students to locate and evaluate sources for further information on the subject.

A deep understanding of America's past is necessary to understand its present and its future. Sometimes you have to look back to see how to best move forward, and that is certainly true when writing the next chapter in the American story.

Setting the Scene:

1770–1793
James Hargreaves invents the spinning jenny, revolutionizing textile manufacturing in England; Eli Whitney invents the cotton gin, creating an explosion of cotton production in the American South.

1861–1865
The American Civil War begins; President Abraham Lincoln issues the Emancipation Proclamation; the Civil War ends with a Union victory; President Lincoln is assassinated.

1770–1793 **1807** **1825** **1844** **1861–1865**

1807
Robert Fulton makes his famous steamboat journey up and down the Hudson River.

1825
The Erie Canal is completed.

1844
Samuel Morse unveils the first working telegraph.

A Timeline

1870
John D. Rockefeller establishes the Standard Oil Company.

1886
The American Federation of Labor, the most influential labor union in U.S. history, is founded.

1939–1945
World War II begins; the United States enters the war; World War II ends with an Allied victory.

1870 | 1886 | 1890 | 1901 | 1909 | 1939–1945

1890
Congress passes the Sherman Antitrust Act, the first major legislation to curb the power of corporations.

1901
The U.S. Steel Corporation is founded.

1909
Henry Ford unveils the Model T automobile.

Introduction

A CENTURY OF ADVANCEMENT

In only 100 years' time, the Industrial Revolution brought about uncountable changes in machines and technology, new sources of energy, and profitable forms of business and trade. The combined impact of these new innovations laid the foundation for modern society as it is now known. In the process, the Age of Industrialization brought the United States—home to the most impressive successes of the time—to its position as one of the foremost superpowers in the world.

The Industrial Revolution began in England in the late 1700s. At that time, motorized machines powered by water, steam, and fossil fuels were being introduced as an alternative to traditional means of production, which had been dependent on the power of physical labor from humans and animals. This revolution in manufacturing spread to other European countries in the early 19th century, but its greatest impact came when it powered its way across the Atlantic Ocean to the United States. The United States was full of ambitious immigrants, the spirit of business, and natural resources. Combined, these elements changed the makeup of America from a largely agricultural society to one dominated by industry in just a few decades. The economic and cultural heartbeat of America shifted from the countryside to the industrial cities that had been small villages just years before. American life changed permanently.

New Fields

The first important industry of this new era was the textile industry because it was in the textile mills of New England that large machines first became a vital part of the manufacturing process. These same mills were also the first American businesses to introduce the

The textile industry was one of the first to boom during the Industrial Revolution.

"factory system" of mass production. Under this system, workers and large machines were brought together in one space, and workers were responsible for specialized jobs in the production process. This type of manufacturing meant that goods were now made in factories, not in homes and workshops, and it quickly spread to other industries. As the 19th century marched on, technological break-throughs, new methods of distribution and management, and the ambitions of wealthy investors brought about a wave of brand new industries. Railroads and steamships chugged across the American landscape, giving farmers, ranchers, manufacturers, and retailers access to markets that lay hundreds of miles away. Steel foundries and oil refineries roared to life, providing essential materials and energy for the creation and operation of massive factories and the sprawling cities those factories inhabited. By the dawn of the 20th century, amazing inventions such as the telephone and the automobile were poised to make their own lasting imprints on American society and business.

Transformations

The astonishing economic impact of the Industrial Revolution was fully matched by its influence on American culture and identity. The wealth it generated gave the United States the ability to conquer and settle the West, thereby extending its borders all the way to the Pacific Ocean. The economic opportunities found in factories and mills convinced millions of immigrants from Europe and other parts of the world to make a new home in America. The inventors and engineers that the revolution inspired brought electrical lighting, indoor plumbing, and other new comforts and conveniences to American families. The Industrial Revolution also gave Americans the means to discover—through travel or newspapers—distant parts of the country that would have otherwise remained complete mysteries. Finally, the Age of Industrialization changed the United States' relationship with the rest of the world. It transformed America into a formidable military power and the planet's leading source of wheat, cotton, coal, oil, and other vital goods by the early 20th century. As one scholar observed, "The industrial revolution constituted one of those rare occasions in world history when the human species altered its framework of existence."[1]

These benefits, however, did not cover up the massive social and economic turmoil that the Industrial Revolution also brought to America. As the 19th century progressed, industrial cities became overcrowded and riddled with political corruption, and many urban neighborhoods deteriorated into slums. Corporation owners took advantage of workers—including children—who worked long hours under hazardous conditions for little pay. Large areas of publicly owned wilderness were sacrificed to the banks, mining companies, railroads, and logging corporations that dominated the nation's economy. The fierce battle for economic advancement, played out on factory floors and in mining camps from the Atlantic states to California, sparked ugly situations of ethnic and racial discrimination and violence.

The Industrial Revolution also contributed to the rise of another ugly institution: slavery. The mechanization of cotton production gave the Deep South a powerful incentive to keep black Americans enslaved. Without slaves to work in the cotton fields, the machines that made cotton the most profitable crop in the world would lie idle and the southern

Large factories, such as this one, became much more common during the Industrial Revolution. This led to a massive increase in production.

economy would fall apart—or so slaveholders argued. The American South thus charted a collision course with the North that culminated in the American Civil War, which ripped across the nation from 1861 to 1865.

Industrial Injustice

By the close of the 19th century, some Americans felt the fast-paced world in which they now lived was ruining the nation's vitality and moral character. "A sense of injustice … had become part of the new glittering, gaudy machine age," wrote one critic. "Machines of steel and copper and wood and stone, and bookkeeping and managerial talent, were creating a new order. It looked glamorous. It seemed permanent; yet … discontent rose in the hearts of the people."[2]

Efforts to address this discontent took many forms in the 20th century, from social reform movements to increased government regulation. However, significant groups in the American public—especially those who were thriving in the new economy—opposed these measures as un-American or anti-business. This philosophical battle continues to rage to this day.

The economic, social, and entrepreneurial forces unleashed by the Industrial Revolution continue to shape the course of American lives. U.S. citizens now live in an era in which the Internet, smartphones, sophisticated home appliances, and nuclear submarines are all taken for granted. However, none of these technological achievements would have come about—at least in the form they take today—were it not for the ambitious inventors and bold entrepreneurs who first brought the Industrial Revolution to life.

Chapter One

THE INDUSTRIAL REVOLUTION: SETTING THE STAGE

Decades before the process of industrialization began to change life in the United States, the age of mechanization and mass production took root in England. In England, the first factories of mass production were opened, and some of the most important inventions of the era, including the steam engine, were introduced. The full potential of these industrial inventions was not realized until they made their way to America, where they became the foundation for an amazing era of social and economic change. This transformation would alter life for Americans—and people all over the world—in ways they never imagined.

The First Modern Industry

The nation of England—along with Wales and Scotland—makes up Great Britain, which is located just off the northern coast of western Europe. In many ways, the country of England that existed in the 18th century provided rich territory for the birth of the Industrial Revolution. The country was blessed with a stable government, a thriving agriculture-oriented economy, a sophisticated banking system, and a culture that encouraged business enterprise. England was sometimes described as a nation of shopkeepers, and this was meant as a compliment. England was also a nation of investors, which proved to be a critical element in the early days of industrialization. These wealthy investors were constantly on the alert for new business opportunities. In the mid-1700s, a series of events in the nation's modest textile industry caught their eye.

Traditionally, the English textile industry was a home-based one in which individual workers took small amounts of fabrics to their homes or shops; created garments, blankets, and other goods on a per-piece basis; and returned the finished product to the manufacturer in exchange for payment. Most of the textiles created under this system were made from wool rather than cotton. In fact, cotton was viewed as a luxury fabric because the natural twist in its fibers made it very time-consuming and difficult to produce.

In the mid-18th century, however, a flurry of inventions forever changed how English textiles were made. The first of these important inventions was the flying shuttle, which was unveiled by John Kay in 1733. This innovation to the loom dramatically increased the speed at which cotton threads could be woven into cloth. This milestone was followed three decades later by the introduction of the spinning jenny, created by James Hargreaves, and the spinning frame, invented by

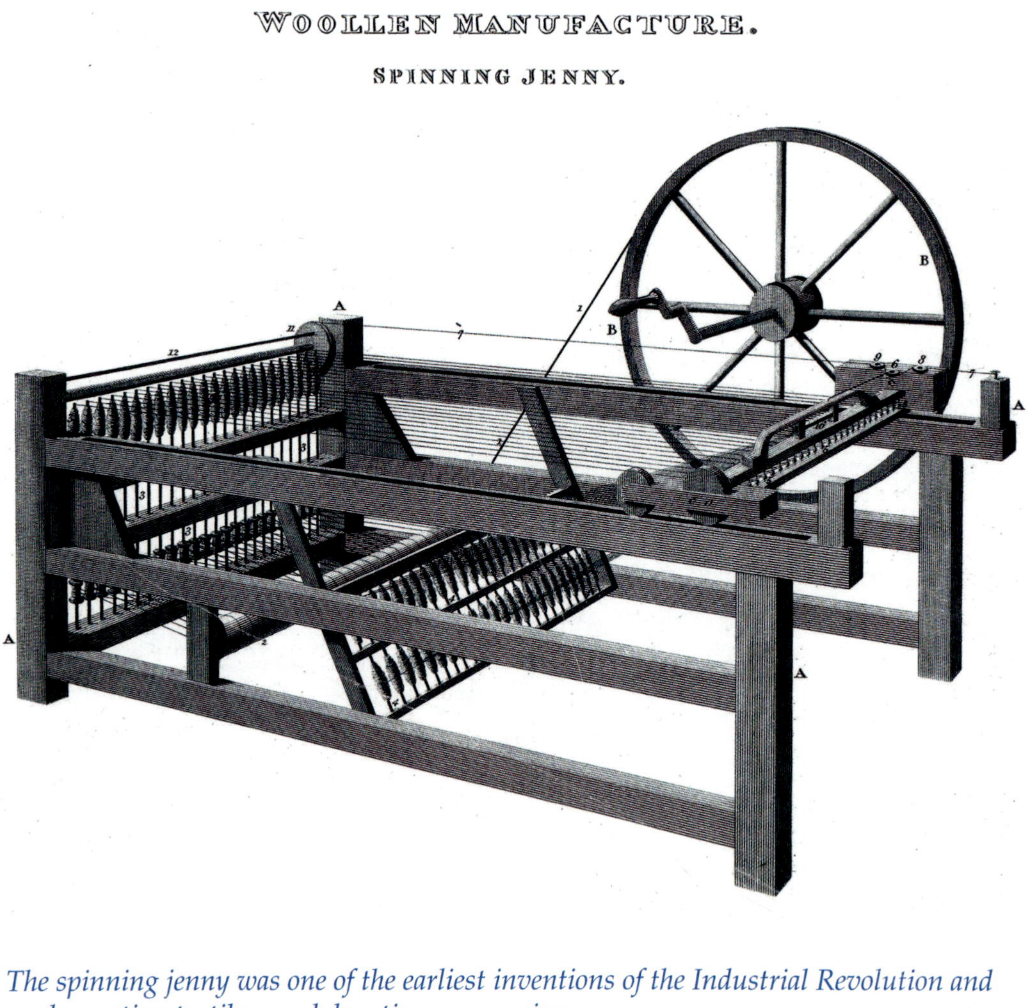

The spinning jenny was one of the earliest inventions of the Industrial Revolution and made creating textiles much less time-consuming.

wigmaker Richard Arkwright. The spinning frame was particularly important because it gave textile makers the first automated process for spinning cotton yarn. With Arkwright's invention, quality clothing and other textiles could be made quickly and inexpensively with cotton, which unsurprisingly, became much more popular with both manufacturers and consumers.

The spinning frame—which later became known as the water frame when Arkwright adjusted his product so that it could be powered by water rather than by hand—made its inventor a very rich man. Gathering investors to his side, Arkwright built a massive cotton mill in Derbyshire, on the banks of the Derwent River, and watched the money come in. "Arkwright lived the life of a feudal lord," wrote one scholar. "The mill was his castle, as carefully guarded as any fortress … He played the lord of the manor … handing out annual prizes to the butchers, bakers, and grocers whom he considered had best served the town."[3] Arkwright established several other water-powered textile mills, and these operations are widely regarded as early examples of the modern industrial factory system.

Profitable Centers of Textile Production

Arkwright was far from the only Englishman to build a fortune out of cotton in the 18th century. The exciting changes in textile manufacturing wrought by the spinning jenny, water frame, and power loom (invented by Edmund Cartwright in 1785) convinced numerous investors to become involved in the industry. Many areas of England, such as the county of Lancashire, experienced an explosion of textile factory construction during the 1770s and 1780s, especially along rivers that could turn the waterwheels of the new mill designs. Once these factories were built, the owners had no trouble piling up orders for their products. "Cotton cloth production increased dramatically," confirmed one economic historian. "In 1765 about five hundred thousand pounds of cotton was spun into thread in Britain, almost all of it at home. Twenty years later sixteen million pounds were spun, mostly in factories."[4]

At times, it seemed that nothing could slow the flood of wealth being generated at these textile mills. Public demand for inexpensive cotton clothing and other materials continued to rise in the early 1800s. The industry was able to meet this demand because it could draw on the large cotton crops generated in India, which was an English colony at the time. In addition, England had large reserves of coal, so when the steam engine replaced water power in the early 1800s, the country's textile makers did not miss a beat.

By the turn of the 19th century, Manchester and other English cities had become the world's leading centers for the manufacture of textiles. Manchester, in fact, had acquired the nickname "Cottonopolis," a tribute to its importance to the global cotton trade. In the process, the textile centers of England also became the first cities in the world to experience the dark side of industrial mass production.

Many mill owners in the United Kingdom ruthlessly exploited the workforce in their quest for riches. Long hours and hazardous working conditions were the rule rather than the exception for the men, women, and children who labored in the factories. One Manchester physician, J.P. Kay, expressed outright horror at the situation. "Whilst the engine runs, the people must work—men, women and children are [tied] together with iron and steam," he described. "[Humans are] chained fast to the iron machine, which knows no suffering and no weariness."[5] Other observers noted that the rapid increase in textile factories had changed huge portions of the English countryside

Updated equipment made textile manufacturing an extremely profitable business.

What Is the Difference?

The nations of England, Wales, and Scotland occupy the North Atlantic island of Great Britain, just off the northern coast of western Europe. These three and the province of Northern Ireland (located on the neighboring island of Ireland) make up the United Kingdom (UK). England is the largest and most heavily populated of the UK's four countries.

The United Kingdom of Great Britain was founded in 1707 by an Act of Union that united the three states into one country with a single Parliament, or government (though Scotland has always kept its own legal system). Nearly 100 years later, in 1801, a new Act of Union joined the neighboring island nation of Ireland to Great Britain. At this point, the full name of the country became the United Kingdom of Great Britain and Ireland. In 1921, however, the Republic of Ireland, which held the majority of the island territory, became independent. Only Northern Ireland remained part of the United Kingdom, so the full name changed to what it is today—the United Kingdom of Great Britain and Northern Ireland.

into harsh metal eyesores and created a lot of waste material.

Such complaints did not convince English factory owners or government officials to address the problems of industrial pollution, child labor, or worker exploitation. They did, however, bring about the birth of the first social reform movements dedicated to changing the darker aspects of industrialization.

The Steam Engine

The second major development in England's Industrial Revolution occurred in 1765, when a Scottish maker of mathematical instruments named James Watt unveiled a new steam engine that could be used for a range of industrial purposes. Watt's invention marked the end of a long quest by European inventors to harness steam for human use. In fact, early experiments in steam power were made in Europe as far back as the 1600s. Not much came of these efforts, though, until 1705, when an English blacksmith named Thomas Newcomen produced a primitive engine that was powered by steam. Within a few decades, steam-powered pumps based on Newcomen's design were being used widely to remove water from English coal-mining pits.

The steam engine design unveiled by Watt was based on Newcomen's engine, but it was far more efficient and sophisticated. Most important, it could be easily modified for use in the textile mills located across England. The arrival of Watt's steam engine, which was fueled by coal, freed mill owners from having to build their facilities on the banks of rivers and streams. Textile factories soon roared to life in regions of England that were far from any river current, and existing mills that invested in the new steam technology were able to expand their production capacity dramatically.

The arrival of this new steam technology sparked economic growth and innovation in other industries across England. In the nation's ironworks, for example, the

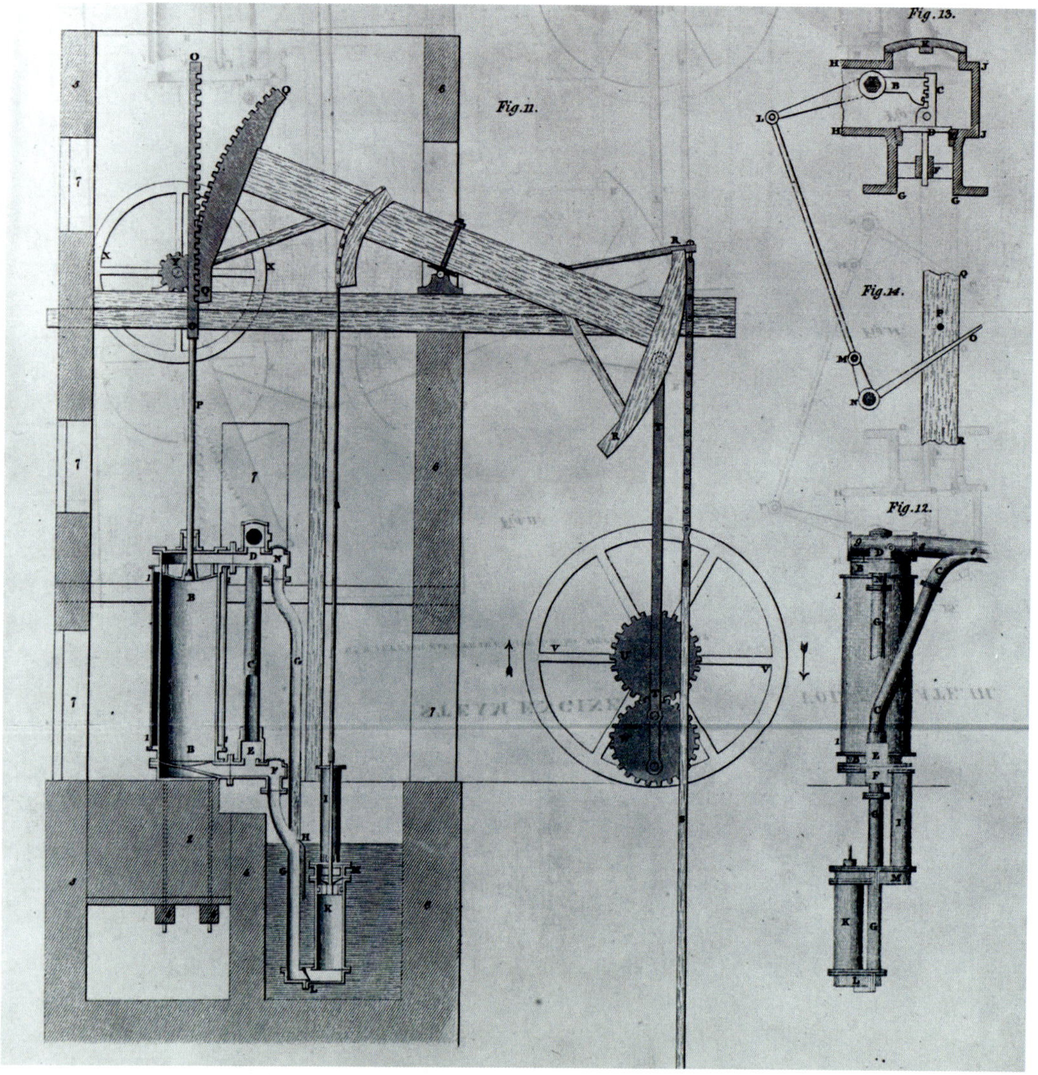

Watt's new steam engine, shown here, allowed factories to move to locations that were not near waterways and increased the productivity of every textile mill that adopted it.

James Watt's Steam-Powered Engines

Born in Scotland in January 1736, James Watt established a thriving mathematical instrument repair shop in Glasgow, Scotland, as a young man. In the early 1760s, he began working on improvements to the steam engine design created by Thomas Newcomen more than a half-century earlier. By 1769, Watt had a patent for his improved design, and a few years later, he entered into a long and profitable partnership with industrialist Matthew Boulton.

During the 1780s and 1790s, Watt made a series of improvements to his steam engine designs, and these found their way into the factories and mines of England. Early in the 19th century, Watt steam engines were exported to the United States in significant numbers. American engineers built on Watt's work to utilize steam as a means to power the steamboats and railroads that became an essential part of the Industrial Revolution in the United States.

Watt retired in 1800, but he continued to tinker with inventions, including a new type of oil lamp. He also traveled throughout western Europe, and even bought an estate in Wales. He died on August 25, 1819, in England.

introduction of steam-powered bellows in blast furnaces helped iron makers switch over from charcoal to coke, an inexpensive by-product of coal. These coke-fired furnaces generated higher temperatures than charcoal, which enabled ironmasters to burn off a greater percentage of imperfections and produce iron products of greater strength and durability. Steam power also freed flour mills from England to Wales from the necessity of building and operating next to waterways. Finally, steam engines became the centerpiece of efforts to make an exciting new mode of transportation—the railroad—more efficient and effective. By the 1820s, steam-powered railways were emerging as an important method of transporting coal—the fuel of industrialization—and other goods to cities and factories in the United Kingdom.

The Birth of the Cotton Gin

One of the most remarkable aspects of the emergence of an Industrial Revolution in England was that it unfolded around the same time the British lost their most prized foreign possession—the colonies in today's United States—in the American Revolution. The successful colonial rebellion that resulted in the establishment of the United States angered the British people. It did not, however, blind them to the potential economic benefits of trade with their former subjects, especially after a young American inventor named Eli Whitney came up with an amazing new invention that turned the textile industry upside down.

A native New Englander, Whitney had only recently graduated from Yale University when he paid a visit to a friend who managed a cotton plantation in Georgia in 1792. During his time in Georgia, he became intrigued by one of the most troublesome problems confronting cotton growers in the South. "[I have] heard much said of the extreme difficulty of ginning [separating seeds from cotton fibers]," he wrote. "There were a number of very respectable Gentlemen … who all agreed that if a machine could be invented which would clean the cotton with [speed], it would be a great thing both to the Country and the inventor. [I] involuntarily happened to be thinking on the subject and struck out a plan for a machine in my mind."[6]

Whitney worked diligently on his invention for the next several months, and in 1793, he revealed his cotton gin. "The machine was simplicity itself," wrote one scholar.

> *Whitney studded a roller with nails, set half an inch apart. When the roller was turned, the nails passed through a grid, pulling the cotton lint from below through the grid, but leaving the seeds behind. A rotating brush swept the lint off the nails into a compartment while the seeds fell into a separate compartment.*
>
> *With Whitney's cotton gin, a laborer could do in a single day what had taken twenty-five laborers to do in that amount of time before.*[7]

When southern planters saw Whitney's cotton gin in action, they rushed to place orders. In a few years, the impact of the invention could be seen throughout the South. Before the cotton gin, America had produced less than one percent of the world's total cotton crop. By the first decade of the 19th century, however, the cotton gin enabled America to compete in the world market. U.S. production continued to surge in the early 1800s, and by 1830, the country was producing unprecedented levels of cotton. Cotton production in the United States rose from about 150,000 bales in 1800 to 4 million bales by 1850.

Cotton Is King

This enormous leap in cotton production would never have occurred if there had not been a market for southern cotton. Factories in the textile centers of England fought to acquire every boll of cotton that the Deep South could squeeze out of the ground. This demand was a great financial advantage to American planters, but it also breathed new life into slavery, which had been fading—both in importance and in practice—across most of America for much of the late 18th century. Just as abolition was gaining some traction because of declining profits in the agricultural South, the increasing profitability of cotton led to a huge demand for slaves.

With each passing year, the cotton-based economy of the American South became more deeply intertwined with slavery. In addition to being a major exporter of cotton, the South of the early 19th century became a major importer of manufactured goods, since it did not invest much in factories that produced these goods. Because of this, the South was a fierce opponent of high taxes on goods received from overseas. The North, on the other hand, was industrializing quickly, so that region of the country favored high taxes, which it believed would protect domestic, or local, manufacturers.

These clashes, however, were

Whitney's cotton gin, shown here, led to the mass production of cotton.

Eli Whitney's Life and Legacy

Eli Whitney was born in Westboro, Massachusetts, on December 8, 1765. After graduating from Yale University in 1792, he visited the American South, where he was inspired to devise a machine to help cotton planters easily separate cotton seeds from the bolls of fiber. His cotton gin provided an enormous boost to American cotton growers. However, it also led the Deep South to become even more deeply reliant on its slave-driven agricultural economy throughout the first half of the 19th century. There are even rumors, still debated among historians, that he took the designs of his groundbreaking invention from some slaves he encountered during his trip.

Whitney hoped to use his cotton gin patent to make himself a wealthy man, but these efforts failed. Patent laws in the United States in the 1790s were weak and rarely enforced, and his cotton gin design was so simple that any skilled craftsman could make one. In the late 1790s and early 1800s, though, he became a successful gun manufacturer. In fact, his gun-making operations introduced the concept of interchangeable parts—triggers and other parts that could be used in multiple models rather than just one product type—to American manufacturing. Whitney died in New Haven, Connecticut, on January 8, 1825.

insignificant compared to the divide between North and South on the issue of slavery. The North-based abolitionist movement condemned slavery as a great moral evil, but many white southerners saw calls to end slavery as a mortal threat to their economy and way of life. Moreover, the importance of cotton to the overall U.S. economy led some southerners to conclude that the North would never try to forcibly end slavery in America. "The slaveholding South is now the controlling power of the world," declared South Carolina senator James Hammond in 1858. "No power on earth dares … to make war on cotton. Cotton is king."[8]

Across the Atlantic Ocean, though, observers in England watched the growing tensions between North and South with alarm. "The lives of nearly two millions of our countrymen are dependent upon the cotton crops of America," wrote the editors of British magazine *The Economist* in 1855. "Should any [disaster] befall the land of cotton, a thousand of our merchant ships would rot idly in dock; ten thousand mills must stop their busy looms; two hundred thousand mouths would starve, for lack of food."[9]

The importance of cotton to the future of the United States was hotly debated in the mid-1800s, when northern and southern states clashed over views on slavery.

Industrialization in America

At the start of the 19th century, England's textile centers and other mechanized industries were the envy of the world. With this in mind, British lawmakers tried to preserve their country's economic advantage over the United States and other nations by passing laws that prohibited the export of textile machinery and textile-related intellectual property. Intellectual property, a term still used today, means creations of the mind with potential economic value, such as inventions, industrial engineering designs, and artistic and literary works. By passing these laws, the British were determined to keep the economic benefits of industrialization to themselves for as long as possible.

These efforts to keep intellectual property within British borders were doomed to fail. For one thing, Americans were determined to build a country that was not dependent on England or any other nation for its economic health and vitality. "Long before Eli Whitney and before the first muskets were drawn at Concord in 1776, the eventual leaders of the new republic realized that to be self-sustaining our citizens would have to dress themselves in native cloth grown and manufactured without any reliance on foreign powers,"[10] wrote one American scholar.

Perhaps even more important, the potential for riches was simply too great to keep ambitious entrepreneurs from figuring out ways to bring England's textile machinery to American shores. In 1790, British immigrant Samuel Slater opened America's first industrial textile mill after completing an apprenticeship at a textile factory in England. The mill was a testament to Slater's powers of memorization; he duplicated virtually every aspect of British textile operations and technology. Today, many economic historians regard the opening of Slater's textile mill as the beginning of America's Industrial Revolution.

Slater's factory was a milestone in American economic history, but an even more important figure in U.S. textiles emerged two decades later. In 1812, Massachusetts native Francis Cabot Lowell returned to the United States after a two-year stay in England. During his visits to Manchester and other industrial centers, Lowell had committed many parts of their rapidly evolving textile operations to memory. Armed with this knowledge, Lowell built textile mills in Waltham, Massachusetts, that integrated all aspects of the cotton manufacturing process—even the dyeing of cloth—under one roof. By the end of the decade, the Waltham mills had grown into America's first corporate empire, and the industrial factory system that had transformed England was firmly established in the U.S. business world.

Chapter Two

AMERICA'S TRANSFORMATION

It only took a few years for big machines, ingenious inventions, and new ways of doing business to transform American life in amazing ways. The early 19th century was an exciting time of industrial growth, and several important factors led to this expansive change. First, America was home to a wide assortment of talented and hard-working inventors and entrepreneurs, as well as a quickly growing workforce that could fill its new factories. Also, it was a young nation with an economic system—capitalism—that encouraged investment and business activity. Finally, the United States had a large amount of natural resources, such as rivers deep and wide enough for ships, huge reserves of coal and other valuable minerals, many trees for wood, and thousands of miles of useable farmland. These raw materials gave American engineers, inventors, and executives the power to make their dreams of industrialization into a reality.

American Confidence and Poise

In England, industrialization had been greeted with distrust and resistance in parts of the country. Many British people liked their traditional way of life, and they feared the impact of the new machines on their jobs and families. These fears about industrialization became even more intense after stories filtered out about the working conditions that evolved in Manchester and other early textile manufacturing centers. By the early 19th century, in fact, English textile workers known as Luddites had even organized violent protests against the mechanized textile mills.

In the United States, machines, factories, and steam power were typically welcomed with open arms. Farmers and city workers alike were happy to have machines that could make their work less exhausting, and business leaders embraced any tool that could increase the output and efficiency of their operations. Consumers also welcomed the promise of greater selection and availability of goods. Lawmakers and community leaders were similarly enthusiastic, for they shared the widespread American belief that their new nation was destined for great things. To many people, the Industrial Revolution seemed like the means by which America would begin charting its course to greatness.

This welcoming attitude mainly came from the fact that the structure of American society was well suited for industrialization. Mechanization and other aspects of industrialization were instantly recognized as keys to greater wealth—the most common way of measuring success in the United States. Talented entrepreneurs and engineers thus flocked to newly mechanized industries.

Finally, the industrialization of American business was aided by the fact that events in England had already done the difficult job of proving that machines

Many Americans welcomed factories, such as the one pictured here, because they liked the benefits that factories could provide.

could improve productivity and profitability. American business leaders knew that industrialization was the wave of the future, and lawmakers at both the state and federal levels did everything in their power to pave the way for investment in industrial machinery and processes. They could also easily draw on the knowledge of British engineers and managers with firsthand experience with the industrialization process. After all, American entrepreneurs and British engineers shared a common language. This made it much easier for U.S. firms to implement the industrial knowledge contained in British trade manuals. Powerful American businessmen also lured British engineers to work for them in the United States, where they accelerated the implementation of industry.

Transportation Across the Nation

Early American industrialism was centered in the northeastern states, which also had the highest concentrations of population in the early 1800s. The metropolitan centers of this region—such as Boston, Massachusetts; Philadelphia, Pennsylvania; and New York City—had lots of workers on hand and supported banks and other sources of investment capital. In addition, all of these cities had access to major waterways, such as rivers, lakes, and the ocean.

The existence of waterways was a huge factor in the economic prospects of any early–19th century American city. Rivers such as the Hudson, Connecticut, Potomac, James, and Susquehanna provided vital waterpower for New England's early textile mills. As time passed and steam power replaced waterpower in American factories, these waterways became more important as transportation routes. Major networks of roadways were nonexistent at the time, and commercially viable railroads had not been invented yet, so rivers, lakes, and coastal waters served as the highways of the nation during the first 50 years of its existence. New York City, for example, became an early center of shipping, banking, and industry because it was built at the juncture of a deep Atlantic harbor and the mighty Hudson River. At the southern end of the country, the same resources—a deep ocean bay and a great river (the Mississippi)—accounted for the emergence of New Orleans as the South's leading center of trade.

In the 1810s and 1820s, American lawmakers and businesspeople tried to make the nation's water-based transportation system more effective by constructing massive canals. These man-made waterways were designed to connect potential farming regions, other landlocked areas of the American interior, and existing waterways with natural river and lake transportation systems.

The most ambitious of these massive canal projects was the Erie Canal in New York State. Construction on the canal began in 1817, when the New York legislature finally authorized the project after years of pressure from supporters such as DeWitt Clinton, a politician who served New York as a U.S. senator, governor, and mayor of New York City. The Erie Canal, Clinton promised, would "convey more riches on its waters than any other canal in the world," transporting resources "to be [spent] in great public improvements; in encouraging the arts and sciences; in patronizing the operations of industry; in fostering the inventions of genius, and in [spreading] the blessing of knowledge."[11]

In 1825—eight years after the massive project broke ground—the Erie Canal's surveyors, engineers, and laborers finally completed their work. The canal stretched 363 miles (584 km) in New York—from the city of Albany (on the Hudson River) to Buffalo (on the shores of Lake Erie). As Clinton had predicted, the canal had an enormous economic impact. It opened a tremendously profitable trade link between eastern population centers such as New York City and the territories of the Great Lakes region. Eastbound shipments of Great Lakes timber, minerals, and crops soared. The holds of westbound ships, meanwhile, were crammed with factory-made textiles and farming tools intended for the migrating families who were pouring into the newly accessible farmlands of the upper Midwest. Many of these changes were evident within a few months of the canal's opening. "It is an impressive sight to gaze up and down the canal," one admirer declared. "In either direction, as far as the eye can see, long lines of boats can be observed. By night, their flickering head lamps give the impression of swarms of fireflies."[12]

The Erie Canal allowed ships to travel from the Atlantic Ocean up the Hudson River and through the canal to the Great Lakes region.

The surge in economic activity from the Erie Canal also sparked explosive growth and economic development in Great Lakes cities, such as Buffalo; Cleveland, Ohio; and Detroit, Michigan, which had been frontier outposts only a few years earlier. In 1820, for example, only a few thousand people lived in Buffalo. Ten years after the canal opened, the city's population stood at more than 20,000 residents, most of whom supported themselves through some aspect of the shipping trade.

The stunning success of the Erie Canal convinced investors, engineers, and lawmakers all across the country to launch canal-building schemes of their own. None of these systems matched the Erie Canal in size and impact, but many had significant regional economic benefits. By 1850, more than 3,700 miles (5,955 km) of canals were built in America. The example of the Erie Canal prompted investment in other public works projects that further fueled America's incredible economic expansion. In the 1850s, for example, the completion of the massive Sault Ste. Marie Canals (also known as the Soo Locks) on the St. Marys River between Lake Huron and Lake Superior opened the entire Superior region for large-scale settlement, development, and commerce.

Full Steam Ahead

The expansion of America's system of navigable waterways took place at the same time that the steam-powered engine was revolutionizing the form and function of the boats that traveled those rivers, canals, and coastal waters. American inventor John Fitch had carried out the first successful experiments with a steam-powered boat in the 1780s and 1790s, but it was not until 1807 that the concept of steam-powered boats and ships really caught the attention of the American public. That year, entrepreneur Robert Fulton took the North River Steamboat 150 miles (241 km) up the Hudson River from New York City, then took a ship full of paying passengers back down to the city.

Fulton's steamboat voyage caused a stir up and down the East Coast. Shipbuilders rushed to build steamboats that could be used to carry freight up and down the nation's rivers. As these vessels joined the bustling water transport system, farmers and factory owners alike marveled at the speed with which steamboats could deliver goods to distant markets. The intense competition between steamer companies, meanwhile, kept shipping charges low for producers and consumers.

Another key milestone in the development of the steamboat—described by one scholar as "the first great American contribution to modern technology"[13]—was the development of a high-pressure steam engine. Fulton and other early steamboat innovators had powered their boats with Watt steam engines, but these engines were not strong enough to power boats along large rivers with strong currents. Steamboats became much more powerful and efficient after Pennsylvania inventor Oliver Evans and Richard Trevithick of Wales—each working independently—developed a high-pressure steam engine in the

Clinton's Ditch

One of the political giants of New York State's history, DeWitt Clinton is known as the father of the Erie Canal. Clinton was born on March 2, 1769, in Little Britain, New York. His uncle was George Clinton, who was the first governor of New York and served as vice president of the United States from 1805 to 1812.

DeWitt Clinton spent his entire adult life in politics. In 1798, he became a member of the New York State Assembly, and he spent the next several years rising through the ranks of state legislators. In 1802, he was elected to the U.S. Senate, but he spent only two years there before beginning a twelve-year term as mayor of New York City. Midway through his tenure as mayor, he ran for president of the United States as the candidate of the Federalist Party, but he was defeated by James Madison.

During his many years as mayor of New York, Clinton became best known as the driving force behind the campaign to build a canal that would connect the Hudson River to Lake Erie. Some critics mocked it, calling it "Clinton's Ditch," but legislative and public support for the project was strong. Thanks to Clinton's tireless support, work began in 1817. When it was completed in 1825, the Erie Canal immediately generated a great surge of economic activity from New York State to the Great Lakes states. Some historians regard it as the single most important public works project in U.S. history.

In 1817—the same year the Erie Canal construction began—Clinton was elected governor of New York. He served three terms as governor, but his third term was cut short when he died on February 11, 1828, in the state capital of Albany.

opening years of the 19th century. "The Watt engine, which had helped to spark the Industrial Revolution and was the most fundamentally important technological development since the printing press three hundred years earlier, was [outdated] after only three decades," observed one scholar. "The pace of change had already begun the relentless acceleration that continues to this day."[14]

Before long, it was clear that a transportation revolution was taking place in America. As one Cincinnati, Ohio, resident stated in 1828, "The steam engine in five years has enabled us to anticipate a state of things, which in the ordinary course of events, it would have required a century to produce."[15] The new high-pressure steam engines established, once and for all, that the

DeWitt Clinton is shown here pouring a keg full of Lake Erie water into the Atlantic Ocean to celebrate the completion of the Erie Canal.

country's mighty rivers were no longer one-way highways. Steam power now gave steamboats the ability to go upstream even against the powerful currents of the Mississippi, Missouri, and Ohio Rivers. As a result, these and other waterways gained more economic importance than ever before. The Mississippi River system, for example, "provided no less than sixteen thousand miles of navigable waters that drained an area of more than a million square miles from western New York State to Montana," noted one historian. "Much of it was the finest agricultural land on earth with almost limitless economic potential. Much of it was also rich in minerals."[16] Steam power unlocked all of these riches for the United States.

Robert Fulton's steamboat aided the transportation of freight and factory goods to locations around the developing nation.

Stable Manufacturing Growth

Advances in steam technology took place against the backdrop of slow but steady growth in factory operations in the United States in the first three decades of the 19th century. Most of this early industrialization continued to take place in New England. It was here that Oliver Evans—the same man who designed the influential high-pressure steam engine—developed fully automated flour mill operations in the 1780s. As one scholar noted, "Until Oliver Evans, no one had conceived of the factory itself as a machine, yet Evans's flour mill was exactly that: You poured grain in one end, and flour came out the other. Except for adjusting, maintaining, and monitoring, the process needed no human labor whatever."[17]

New England was also the region where America's first great industry, textile manufacturing, was centered. In 1830, textile factories still dominated the

Robert Fulton's Steamboat

Steamboating icon Robert Fulton ranks as one of the most legendary figures in American business history. He did not actually invent the steamboat, as is commonly believed, but he proved it could be effectively used for moneymaking purposes. In addition, Fulton's fleet of New York City–based steamers made his business enterprise one of the first major transportation corporations in the United States.

Fulton was born on November 14, 1765, in Lancaster County, Pennsylvania. As a young man, he briefly pursued a career as a painter. By the early 1790s, he had shifted his attention to industrial and mechanical engineering. He first devoted his talents to building canals and drafting experimental submarine designs. In 1802, he formed a business partnership with Robert Livingston, a U.S. diplomat who held an exclusive right to operate steam-driven boats in New York State for a 20-year period.

Financed by Livingston, Fulton experimented with steamboat designs first created by fellow American John Fitch. In 1807, he unveiled a steam-powered boat named the North River Steamboat. This vessel was a commercial success, and it ushered in an age of steamboat travel across America. Fulton spent the next several years designing new steamboats, building steam engines at an engine works in New Jersey, and amassing a fortune from his partnership with Livingston. He died on February 24, 1815.

Robert Fulton was one of the most important early engineers of the Industrial Revolution.

U.S. economic landscape. Between 1820 and 1840, there was a massive surge of industrial investment along the East Coast. Some of this financing came from British business interests, but overall, the increase was from domestic businessmen. American lawmakers in local, state, and federal governments provided all sorts of economic aid to industrializing businesses, including tax exemptions and special arrangements to limit competition. They wanted the economy to thrive.

State governments were particularly energetic in funding and starting businesses and other public improvements. Between 1816 and 1826, for example, lawmakers in Ohio established 18 turnpikes, 7 bridges, 2 harbors, 7 banks, 1 insurance company, 1 waterworks, and other public works projects. Banks emerged as a major investing force in American business during this era. Some of this investment capital went into textiles, of course, but a lot was directed to new industries, such as steam shipping, railroads, and various manufacturing areas.

These factors contributed to a decade of tremendous manufacturing expansion in the 1840s. Factories that produced all sorts of goods—some intended for household use, others for use in business operations—multiplied across the eastern half of the United States. Smaller factories began to appear in the American West, where the steamboat had opened new opportunities for farmers and mining interests. "The steamboat appeared as an angel of deliverance [to western communities]," wrote one historian. "Steam did not wholly banish muscle power from the western rivers. But it reawakened visions of accelerating development and gave new reign to prophecies of western greatness."[18]

By the early 1850s, American factories were producing so many innovative and useful products in such great volumes that England—the original home of the Industrial Revolution—began conducting studies of the U.S. manufacturing system. These reports marveled at the speed with which small U.S. shops and mills were expanding into major employers. They also reported on the enormous amount of economic activity that was taking place in America. They admitted it would be difficult for England to duplicate such success, for the United States simply had more people and natural resources.

Fueling the Industrial Revolution

One of the most important natural resources that drove America's rapid industrialization was coal. The steam engines that powered factories and steamships needed fuel. As the 19th century progressed, coal increasingly replaced wood as the fuel of choice. It also became the main heating fuel for households across much of America.

The first great center of coal production was Pennsylvania, which held massive deposits of high-quality anthracite coal and lower-quality bituminous coal. During the 1820s, coal-mining activity transformed Pittsburgh from a small village into a bustling city full of

Many young boys, similar to the ones pictured here, were hired to work in mines to satisfy the nation's need for coal.

glassmakers and ironworks—both fuel-intensive industries heavily dependent on coal. In addition, by 1845, millions of tons of anthracite coal had been transported out of the hills of western Pennsylvania via steamboat and railroad to factories and households along the East Coast. In fact, western Pennsylvania produced more anthracite coal than the rest of the country combined by the mid-1800s, and it employed a huge portion of the total coalmining workforce.

Anthracite coal was essential in the development of the railroad industry. It ranked as a major source of income for virtually all midcentury railroad companies, as their trains delivered the coal around the country. Its importance to the iron industry also made it essential for the overall buildup of the railroad industry's infrastructure. During the 1830s and 1840s, innovative processes of smelting iron from anthracite coal enabled iron makers to dramatically expand production of high-quality, reasonably priced iron rails and other materials essential to railroads. Not surprisingly, several leading railroad companies of this era became major players in the coal industry. "Anthracite country is often called the cradle of American railroading, and with good reason," explained one historian.

> *The anthracite mine operators were the first Americans to use rails, and they greatly advanced the science of building railways …The Philadelphia and Reading Railroad, one of the nation's largest and most powerful companies, dominated the area, but there would be five railways so intermingled with the anthracite trade that coal and railroading were often considered a single industry.*[19]

An Iron Transformation

Ironically, these industrial advances might have happened sooner if not for the fact that U.S. iron makers were slow to embrace certain technological innovations. In the 1820s, British iron makers had introduced the coal-fired blast furnace. These coal-fired forges generated higher temperatures than charcoal, a lower-quality but easily obtainable fuel that had long been used in the industry. The higher temperatures enabled iron makers to burn off a greater percentage of carbon and thus produce iron products of superior strength and durability.

Within a few years, Great Britain's iron industry had used this technology to move to the forefront of the world's iron producers. In fact, the nation became an exporter of iron after years of being an importer. In the United States, foundry and forge owners stubbornly maintained their loyalty to the charcoal-based production system that the British had abandoned.

The American iron industry was slow to follow the British example for two reasons. First, the U.S. government had attached heavy tariffs on iron imports from England. These taxes made American iron less expensive than English iron. In addition, the demand for iron goods was so extraordinarily high across the country that forge owners did not have to worry about producing works of premium quality on a timely basis. They knew that virtually everything they produced—from firearms to stoves to parts for ships and locomotives—would be purchased as soon as it appeared on the market.

In the 1830s, though, U.S. iron makers began to invest in the blast-furnace technology that had been such an

Innovative new approaches to the iron industry helped increase the production, quality, and profitability of iron.

advantage to the British. Forge owners who made the switch from charcoal to coal were enormously successful. Their output was mostly responsible for the sharp increase of U.S. iron production during the 1840s. The changing competitive environment forced some smaller and less efficient iron makers out of business. Large corporations with impressive arrays of forges and rolling mills assumed greater prominence. These corporations entered the 1850s in good shape to meet the business challenges and opportunities associated with the impending opening of the West to settlement and development.

Changes in Farming Routines

As the first half of the 19th century drew to a close, industrialization was transforming the lives—and livelihoods—of farmers who lived far from the bustling factories, railroad yards, and crowded immigrant neighborhoods of expanding cities.

America had been a land of farmers since the colonial era, and agriculture remained the leading area of economic activity well into the Age of Industrialization. Some farming families viewed the economic and social changes brought by the Industrial Revolution with greater fear and skepticism than their urban counterparts. However, others seized the new economic opportunities that came with industrialization, such as increased access, via railroads and steamships, to markets that lay hundreds or thousands of miles away. Farmers would never have been able to meet the needs of the rapidly growing population of the United States—or meet the growing demand for cotton and other crops overseas—if they had not embraced industrialization in their own operations.

The first major technological innovation that shaped American agriculture was Eli Whitney's cotton gin. When it was introduced in the 1790s, this revolutionary tool made cotton production a much more efficient and profitable enterprise. It single-handedly turned the economy of the American South into one that was overwhelmingly dependent on cotton. Unfortunately, the stunning growth in demand for cotton—a labor-intensive crop—made white southern commerce and culture more dependent on slavery than ever before. This state of affairs put the South in conflict with the North, which had developed a very different economic and industrail system by the 1800s.

Other technological advances in the field of agriculture had fewer controversial side effects than the cotton gin. In fact, most of them were embraced because they made the tasks of raising and harvesting crops less difficult and time-consuming than they had been for previous generations. Agricultural machinery, such as William Pennock's 1841 grain drill and John Deere's 1837 wrought-iron plow, enabled farmers to sow seeds much more quickly, while threshing machines introduced in the 1830s and 1840s dramatically cut harvesting time.

Sowing and Reaping

The single most important mechanical tool to appear on farms in the 19th century was Cyrus McCormick's mechanical reaper. McCormick's reaper, which he first displayed in 1831, mechanized every component of the wheat harvesting process, and it freed farmers and hired hands from the slow, exhausting task of reaping wheat with handheld tools.

McCormick's machine was so large in size and revolutionary in its capabilities that farmers refused to try it at first. They assumed it could not work as well as promised. The inventor failed to sell a single reaper for years, and in the early 1840s, he was still selling only a handful each year. It took until 1845 for McCormick's fortunes to change. When poor weather produced grain crop failures across Great Britain, authorities responded to the disaster by removing several laws that had prevented U.S. farmers from selling wheat in Great Britain. As wheat growers scrambled to meet the soaring demand for their product, they turned to McCormick, who had built a factory in Chicago, Illinois, for the mass production of his harvesters. Within a decade, McCormick harvesters were rumbling across farms from Ohio to the western edge of the Great Plains. "With

Cyrus McCormick's mechanical reaper was one of the most important pieces of farming technology in history.

McCormick Reaps the Benefits

Inventor Cyrus McCormick was born in Virginia on February 15, 1809. He spent his youth working on his father's grain and livestock farm. The long hours he spent cutting wheat by hand made an impression on him. In 1831, the 22-year-old invented a mechanical reaping machine that could harvest wheat far more swiftly and efficiently than could be accomplished by manual labor.

McCormick struggled to sell his invention for the next several years. By the late 1840s, though, wheat growers were so eager to increase their yields and streamline their operations that they began to buy McCormick's reaper in large numbers. McCormick kept up with the rising demand by establishing a factory in Chicago that mass-produced them. The distribution of these reapers across America's heartland has been cited as a major factor in the surge in U.S. wheat production that began in the 1850s.

By the mid-1850s, McCormick was a millionaire. He invested heavily in Chicago real estate and U.S. railroads, and he expanded his reaper sales into Europe. After his death in 1884, his son Cyrus Jr. took over the business. In 1902, the company merged with four other makers of agricultural machine products to create a giant firm, International Harvester. This company remained one of the largest agricultural equipment companies in the world throughout the 20th century.

McCormick's reaper, one man could harvest eight acres a day, not one, and the American Middle West could become the bread basket of the world," wrote one historian.

The McCormick reaper not only greatly enlarged the potential size of American grain crops, it changed how Americans have earned their livelihoods. With the introduction of the reaper and the endless parade of mechanical agricultural equipment that followed, the percentage of American workers engaged in agriculture has steadily declined, even while agricultural output has continued to grow. The McCormick reaper thus helped crucially to supply the labor needed in the great expansion of American industry that followed the Civil War.[20]

Chapter Three

THE GOLDEN AGE OF THE INDUSTRIAL REVOLUTION

During the second half of the 1800s, the Industrial Revolution hit its peak. This was a time in which industrial marvels, economic growth, and expansion into new lands all seemed to march together into a golden age. The United States reached new heights of wealth, opportunity, and power, all within a few decades. The steam-powered railroad, which is perhaps the most important invention of the 19th century, was crucial to this expansion and growth. Other major inventions and innovations—from the telegraph to mass production of steel—also occurred during this era. By the end of the 1800s, these interdependent industries had made the United States a global economic power and a force to be reckoned with—all while ushering in the age of the modern corporation.

Railroads Chug onto the Scene

The first railroads advanced enough to be used for profitable commercial activity appeared in the late 1820s and early 1830s. England's first practical railroad was George Stephenson's Liverpool and Manchester Railway, which began operating in 1830. Not long after, the Baltimore and Ohio (B&O) Railroad established itself as the first successful steam-powered railroad company in the United States. Neither of these railroads—or the ones that soon followed—were based on the work or invention of a single individual. Rather, they were the result of the collective efforts of many engineers and inventors who mastered different components of railroad design and operation.

Unlike canals, rivers, and rough roadways, railroads could be built nearly anywhere, and they could operate year-round in all kinds of weather. These characteristics made the railroad a wonderful resource for transporting freight from one place to another and gave travelers a speedy and comfortable transportation alternative to canals and rough roads. These advantages were clear to U.S. engineers and investors, who gathered around the new technology. In 1830, the railroad industry barely existed. One decade later, however, nearly 3,000 miles (4,828 km) of track had been laid across the United States, mostly in the East. By 1850, more than 9,000 miles (14,484 km) of railroad lines snaked across America, and by the time the Civil War erupted in 1861, more than 30,000 miles (48,280 km) of lines had been built. Most of these lines were in the North, which gave the Union a tremendous military advantage during the war.

Many railroad lines built in the 1840s and 1850s connected cities to other cities, but others were built to link mining facilities and timber tracts to factories and mills. Wherever they were constructed, railroads changed America's social, business, and environmental landscape in lasting ways. In some respects, their legacy was a positive one, but they also

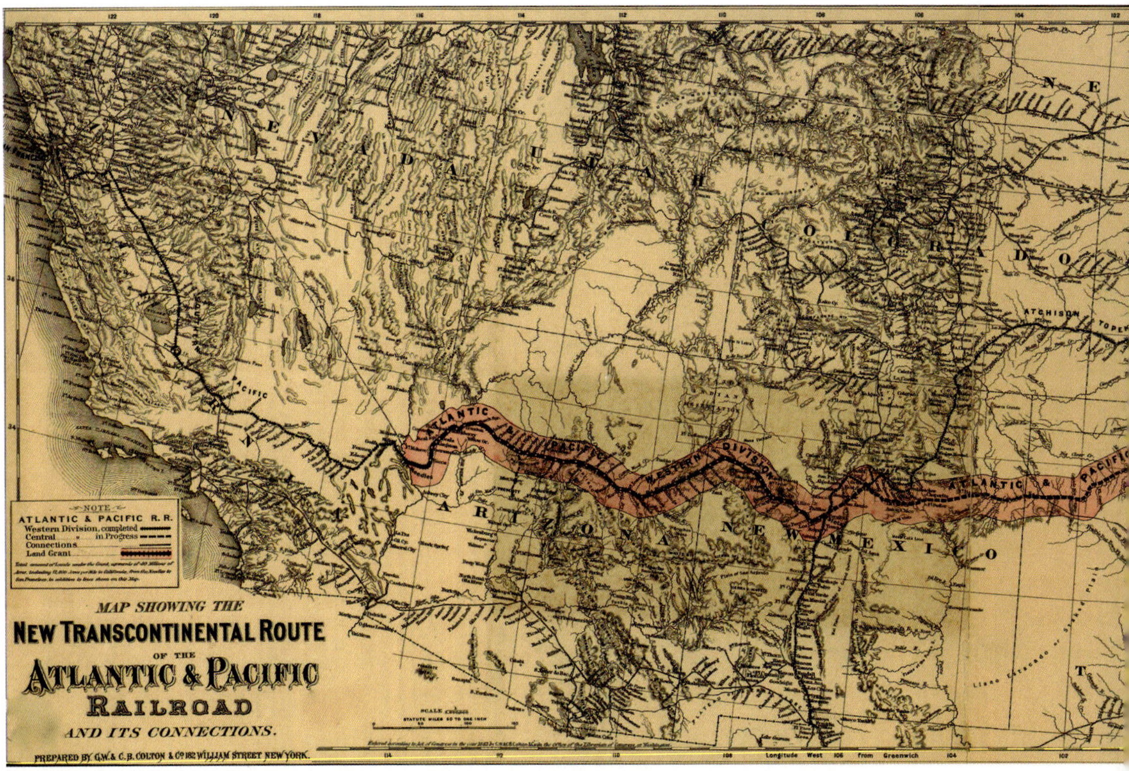

This map shows the route of the original transcontinental railroad, built by the Central Pacific and Union Pacific companies, which connected the United States across thousands of miles of wilderness.

had a dark side. For example, railroads gave rural farmers, ranchers, and mining companies access to markets they never had before, but they also crushed steamboat operations that had been raking in profits in the pre-railroad era. Cities and towns blossomed along rail lines and pulsed with economic activity, but this gave railroad owners extreme power over the future of entire communities. A town could see its population explode in a short time if a rail line was built through it—but if that rail line stopped running, the population would vanish. The city would be left to pay the price.

The railroad also went a long way toward making the ever-growing United States feel like a unified country, rather than a vast collection of remote communities. However, in many regions of the country, the forces it unleashed had a destructive impact on the environment. Entire forests were carried away on the backs of railroads. Towns and cities nurtured by the railroads turned the surrounding countryside into wheat fields, grazing lands, and industrial sites. Altogether, these swift economic and cultural changes prompted one visitor to America, English writer William Makepeace Thackeray, to comment, "We who have lived before the railways were made, belong to another world."[21]

Finally, railroads were the first U.S. industry to introduce modern management principles to their operations. By midcentury, railroad companies had become so large and had established offices over such vast geographical areas that they were forced to adopt organizational structures with clear lines of authority and responsibility. These structures, which were led by large numbers of salaried officers and managers, eventually filtered into the steel industry and other major industries that emerged in the late 19th century.

Settling the West

The railroad was a vital instrument of western settlement. During the first half of the 19th century, the United States used the Louisiana Purchase of 1803, the treaty that ended the Mexican-American

War, and land cessions from Britain to expand its territory from the eastern banks of the Mississippi River all the way to the Pacific Ocean. Most Americans were convinced it was God's will that they tame this vast wilderness, defeat the Native American inhabitants, and use the region's natural resources to improve their own lives. The belief that Americans were fated to conquer and settle the West became known as Manifest Destiny.

White settlers flooded into the West in the second half of the 19th century. Eager to make better lives for themselves and their families, these pioneers took advantage of cheap land grants and other government programs designed to encourage settlement of the West. They established farms, mining operations, towns, and cities in places that had been Native American hunting grounds only a few years earlier. By the close of the 19th century, the vast lands between the Pacific Ocean and Mississippi River supported cities and industries that rivaled the greatest cities of the East. "For all the men who were broken and women who were dried to leather by the frontier, for all the slaughter and waste of resources, for all the unrealized dreams, the promise of the West was nevertheless fulfilled,"[22] described one observer of the era.

The transformation of the West would never have been possible, though, without the "iron horse," as the railroad was called in frontier communities. This transportation option had transformed the economy and culture of the eastern United States in the 1830s and 1840s, and it did the same thing in the West in the second half of the century. Vast networks of railroad lines moved settlers from the East to the West and gave manufacturers and farmers the means to send their products greater distances. Railroads greatly increased the speed by which everything—from iron ore to information—could be delivered cross-country. "Lumber, coal, glass, iron, construction, and lubrication businesses located anywhere near the new [rail] lines prospered in their wake," affirmed one historian. "Bankers, brokers, printers, newspaper editors, whalers, even sandwich-makers, cashed in on the new riches. Railways equally benefited shippers, importers and exporters, manufacturers, miners, farmers, and almost every other occupational group imaginable."[23]

In many cases, railroad companies took an even more active role in distributing western lands than state, territorial, or federal authorities. During the construction of the transcontinental railroad, for example, the federal government authorized the distribution of 33 million acres (13 million ha) of public land to railroad companies along the route. The government gave up these lands to incentivize the construction of the railroad, and the Union Pacific and Central Pacific—the two companies that built it—were free to use the land for whatever purpose they wanted. Most of the time, the land was used for its natural resources, though the companies also sold it to settlers and towns looking to expand westward.

Land grant programs were essential in the settlement and development of the Great Lakes region, but they were even more important in spurring settlement in the West. Congress and various state and territorial governments granted western railroads a total of about 116 million acres (47 million ha) in land grants. Four railroads—the Northern Pacific; the Atchison, Topeka and Santa Fe; the Union Pacific; and the Southern Pacific—received roughly 70 percent of the total land awarded. These distributions of public land gave the railroads a huge economic incentive to tame the West. "Railroad companies, especially those possessing land grants, were colonizers of the Great Plains on a big scale," one scholar explained. "They carried forward on a vast scale the work that had been done on a lesser scale by colonizing companies on the seaboard in the colonial period."[24]

Over time, the railroads became so closely associated with the health and life of the growing American empire that many people used the language of mythology to describe the trains roaring across the countryside. Asa Whitney, who

The companies that created the transcontinental railroad in the 1860s built trestles such as this to cross the difficult lands of the West.

Luring Settlers

Of all the land distribution programs instituted to encourage Western settlement, none was as important as the Homestead Act of 1862. It was specifically created to attract settlers to territory that opened as a result of the passage of the Kansas-Nebraska Act of 1854. According to the terms of this act, any U.S. citizen or immigrant who was white, male, and 21 years old or the head of a family could take possession of 160 acres (65 ha) of unsettled public land by paying a small claim fee. So long as he promised to live on the land for at least five years and improve it, such as by cultivating crops or building a home, he would receive final title at no additional cost. Later changes to the act increased the size of the grant to 640 acres (259 ha) and shortened the necessary period of residence.

The Homestead Act enabled millions to successfully establish themselves in the West. However, the inexpensive terms of the act hid the true cost of pursuing a new life in the western states and territories. Much of the land that was available through the act was not suitable for raising crops or livestock because timber and mining companies and wealthy cattle ranchers were able to use their political connections to quickly claim the best land. In addition, many poor farmers were at the mercy of forces beyond their control, such as weather and railroad freight rates.

helped build the nation's first transcontinental railroad in the 1860s, declared that when traveling by train, "time & space are annihilated by steam, we pass through a City a town, [even] a country, like an arrow from Jupiters Bow."[25] In 1853, one writer described the American train as

> *the earth-shaker, the fire-breather, which tramples down the hills, which outruns the [slow] winds, which leaps over the rivers, which grinds the rocks to powder and breaks down the gates of the mountains … Shall not cities be formed from his … breath, and men spring up from the cinders of his furnace? [History will remember] how Senatorial thunders … at last by [great] force broke down the wall, and rode through in triumph on the Iron Horse.*[26]

Crops and Farming

As railroad routes sprouted across the country and more land was converted

Settlers on homesteads, such as this family, left the East for the West. Between 1862 and 1900, numerous families received cheap land from the government.

for agricultural use, the United States experienced a massive increase in crop production. Between 1870 and 1900, the total number of farms more than doubled. The total amount of land set aside for farming expanded dramatically during these decades.

Not surprisingly, this expansion in land under cultivation and the arrival of mechanized farming—as well as more sophisticated use of fertilization and irrigation techniques—generated huge jumps in the agricultural industry. Wheat production increased from 250 million to 600 million bushels between 1870 and 1900, and corn production rose from 1.1 million to 2.7 million bushels in this same time period. Cotton production in the post–Civil War era surged as well. As the Reconstruction era gave way to discriminatory Jim Crow laws across the Deep South, white planters reasserted their power over poor white and black sharecroppers. By the close of the 19th century, these economically penniless and politically powerless

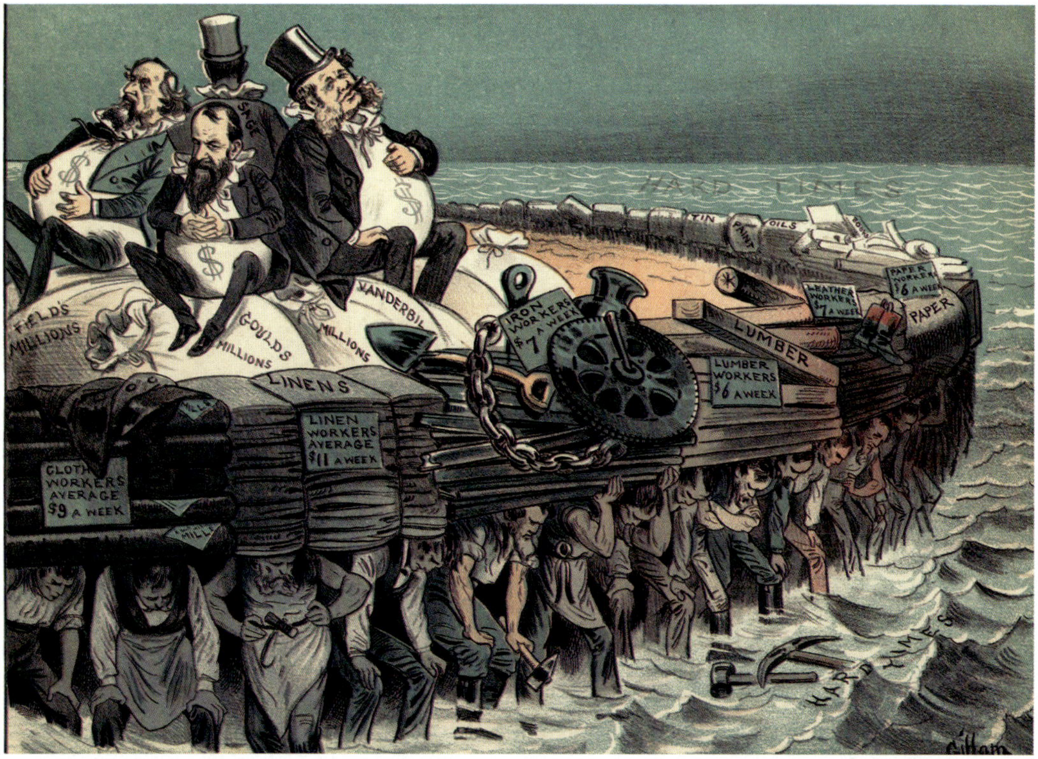

Many people were angry about the rise of robber barons. This political cartoon shows laborers in a sea of hard times struggling to hold up lumber, paper, and many other industries with low-wage jobs as the industrialists and their millions of dollars weigh them down.

sharecroppers were helping to produce more than 10 million bales a year for the southern cotton lords.

Investment capital and settlement patterns established manufacturing in towns and cities that had been little more than trading posts a few decades earlier. Many textile operations gradually drifted out of New England to the South, where the costs of hiring workers and shipping cotton were much lower. Meanwhile, factories and mills followed the millions of settlers who had been attracted to the West by reports of gold, promises of farmland, or steady work in timber and mining camps.

All of this economic activity and political influence turned the nation's leading railroad owners, financiers, and mining executives into wealthy and powerful men. Some of these men, such as Jay Gould, Cornelius Vanderbilt, John D. Rockefeller, and J.P. Morgan, became household names. However, fame did not translate into respect among the general public. In fact, railroad magnates and other industrial tycoons became known as "robber barons"—a negative term that reflected the belief that these men built their fortunes through ruthless exploitation of workers, cunning manipulation of lawmakers and officials, and savage attacks on competitors.

Coal and Oil

The robber barons were aware of their reputation, but they paid little attention to how average Americans viewed them. Instead, they maintained their focus on advancing industrialization and increasing the riches that could be gained from it. One of their highest priorities was finding new energy sources to feed the factories, foundries, and railroads of the Industrial Revolution. Two substances—coal and oil—emerged as the precious fuels of the Industrial Age.

In colonial America, and for much of the pre–Civil War era, most of the nation's energy needs had been met with wood. Locomotives and household stoves alike were fueled in this manner. Most Americans were unaware not only of coal's superior qualities as a source of heat and energy, but also of the vast tracts of coal that existed in the hills of Pennsylvania and other parts of the country.

The appetite for firewood was so great, in fact, that its impact on forests was far greater than timber cutting for building lumber. The incredible rate of deforestation alarmed some Americans, who urged their fellow citizens to take better care of the wilderness. Despite this, most Americans ignored such warnings because they believed that the supply of land and resources within the nation's borders was inexhaustible.

After the Civil War, though, coal consumption steadily increased. The inexpensive mineral was ideally suited for use in industrial forges, and it became the preferred energy source in many households. In the mid-1880s, coal surpassed wood as the nation's leading energy source. Virtually all of this coal came from domestic sources, as mining companies tapped into vast deposits in Pennsylvania, West Virginia, and Ohio, as well as Colorado and other western states.

By the beginning of the 20th century, Americans from Maine to California recognized that the nation's economic future was heavily dependent on coal production. Coal's main rival as a source of energy was oil. In the 1840s, the oil industry barely existed. When engineers developed new ways of accessing oil in the 1850s and inventors quickly figured out new uses for it, the industry exploded. By the 1870s, a byproduct of oil, called kerosene, replaced whale oil as the nation's main fuel for lanterns, and oil refineries developed forms of gasoline that were used as fuel oils, solvents, and lubricants. In the 1880s and 1890s, the oil industry emerged as a major economic force in the United States. This emergence was due partly to steadily rising demand for oil and partly to the uniting of the oil industry in the hands of one brilliant and ruthless entrepreneur: John D. Rockefeller.

Rockefeller had entered the oil business in the early 1860s as a minor investor. By the end of the 1880s, though, he had built his Standard Oil Company

A Dark Reputation

Even among the corporate giants and financiers that the public named robber barons, the industrialist Jason "Jay" Gould had a dark reputation. Born in Roxbury, New York, on May 27, 1836, Gould left the family farm to work as a surveyor, clerk, and blacksmith. In the early 1860s, he moved to New York City and became active in the stock market. Within a few years, he manipulated stock in small railroads and other companies so effectively that he became a wealthy man.

Ambitious and competitive, Gould dove deeper into the worlds of stocks and railroads. In the late 1860s and 1870s, he organized a series of shady business deals, including a bold scheme to corner the gold market in 1869. This particular plan backfired when Gould's maneuvering triggered a panic on Wall Street that sent all stocks, including ones that he owned, plummeting. However, his many other stock manipulation schemes enabled him to recover his losses and add to his fortune within a few years.

In the 1870s, Gould concentrated on building up his railroad investments. By 1881, he controlled a railroad empire that included profitable lines across the country, and his warlike attitude toward competing railways was known far and wide. He also seized a controlling stake in Western Union, the greatest of the telegraph companies that emerged in the post–Civil War era. In these and many other business dealings, he became notorious as a ruthless double-crosser who tried to squeeze every last cent of profit out of every man he employed.

By the time Gould died on December 2, 1892, he was universally regarded as one of the most hated men in America. As biographer Maury Klein wrote, "Two generations of operators, businessmen, bankers, lawyers, coupon clippers, stockholders, politicians, reformers, journalists, ministers, and other guardians of the public morals reviled him as the supreme villain of his age."[1]

1. Maury Klein, *The Life and Legend of Jay Gould*. Baltimore, MD: Johns Hopkins University Press, 1986, p. 3.

into a financial empire without equal in the United States. It was the dominant producer, refiner, and seller of oil across the country. By the close of the 19th century,

> *Standard Oil seemed omnipotent [all-powerful]. Everything about its operation was colossal: Twenty thousand wells poured their output into 4,000 miles of Standard Oil pipelines, carrying the crude to seaboard or to*

5,000 Standard Oil tank cars. The [combined companies] now employed 100,000 people and [oversaw] the export of 50,000 barrels of oil daily. Rockefeller's creation could be discussed only in superlatives: It was the biggest and richest, the most feared and admired business organization in the world.[27]

Strong as Steel

America's switch to coal and oil was of enormous benefit to the nation's iron industry, which used a series of innovations to transform itself into a maker of steel in the 1860s and 1870s. Prior to the Civil War, the United States produced less than 12,000 tons (10,886 mt) of steel annually. Steelmaking was expensive and time-consuming, so the substance generally was reserved for special products, such as prairie plows and fine-edged tools.

In the 1860s, though, the Bessemer steelmaking process was introduced in iron foundries in England and the United States. This technological advance was named after Sir Henry Bessemer of England, but an American ironmaster named William Kelly actually made the same breakthrough at roughly the same time. Both men discovered a method of creating steel by using air to remove excess carbon and other impurities in molten iron. Armed with this innovation,

The Bessemer process transformed the steel industry from time-intensive to efficient and dramatically increased the demand for steel.

iron makers were able to process steel in far greater volumes than ever before.

Steel was a much stronger and more reliable product than iron, so when steel production became commercially viable, the impact was felt across the U.S. economy. Steel became the material of choice for railroad lines and the skyscrapers that rose in numerous cities. By 1880, annual American steel production reached an incredible 1.2 million tons (1.1 million mt)—100 times more than the industry was producing only 20 years earlier. During this time, the industry became one of the country's leading employers of Irish, German, Russian, Italian, Polish, and English immigrants. As one historian noted, "A vast pool of unskilled labor lay only an ocean away [and] the steel mills of America soon exerted a strong gravitational pull on the European masses."[28]

Many of these immigrants went to work for Andrew Carnegie. The Carnegie Steel Company, which was led by Carnegie and his partner Henry Clay Frick, had been carefully constructed in the 1870s and 1880s so that it had a presence in every aspect of the steel industry. Carnegie's personal secretary, James Howard Bridge, recalled that by the early 1890s, the Carnegie steel empire

> *owned its own mines, dug its ore with machines of amazing power, loaded it into its own steamers, landed it at its own ports, transported it on its own railroads, distributed it among its many blast furnaces, and smelted it with coke similarly brought from its own coal-mines and ovens, and with limestone brought from its own quarries. From the moments these crude stuffs were dug out of the earth until they flowed in a stream of liquid steel into the ladles, there was never a price, profit, or royalty paid to an outsider.*[29]

By the end of the 19th century, Carnegie Steel was not only America's leading steelmaker, it also was producing more steel than the entire British steel industry.

Economic Interdependence

The rise of Carnegie Steel and the rest of the U.S. steel industry could never have occurred without coal's emergence as a foundry fuel. Nor could the steel industry have risen to the heights it did if America's railroads had not developed such an enormous appetite for steel rails. These realities show that America's Industrial Revolution was based on various industries working together. The steel industry, for example, had an enormous influence on the real estate industry; it provided developers with the raw material to construct the railroad depots, dams, harbors, bridges, factories, and office buildings that became the foundations of modern American cities. Similarly, western cattle ranching became much more profitable after the 1870s, when refrigerated railcars made it much easier to deliver beef to market.

In addition, one historian noted that the needs of the railroad

The Man Behind the Telegraph

Samuel Finley Breese Morse was born on April 27, 1791, in Charlestown, Massachusetts. The son of a minister, he attended Yale University and spent several years studying painting in England. Morse eventually established a thriving portrait studio in Boston. In the early 1830s, he became fascinated with early experiments with electromagnetism, which some scientists believed could be harnessed to send messages long distances over wire.

Morse teamed with Alfred Vail to build a telegraph prototype that could transmit electrical pulses of varying length—an alphabet of dots and dashes that came to be known as Morse code—over electrical wires to stations miles apart. Morse received a patent for his telegraph invention in 1837, and in 1843, he received a long-sought grant from the U.S. Congress to build a telegraph line between Washington, D.C., and Baltimore, Maryland. Several months later, on May 24, 1844, he successfully transmitted a message between the Washington and Baltimore stations. Word of this triumph triggered a frenzy of telegraph network building up and down the East Coast.

During the second half of the 19th century, Morse's invention spread across the United States and changed American life forever. It also made the inventor a wealthy man. In his later years, Morse divided his time between charitable efforts, political activism, and his large family. He died in New York City on April 2, 1872.

industry sustained a wide assortment of manufacturers:

> *Railroads required enormous quantities of industrial goods: locomotives, freight and passenger cars, rails, cross ties, spikes, and bridge members, to name just a few. At first, nearly all these had to be imported from England. But as the American demand for these commodities grew, more and more American entrepreneurs began to supply them, driving the Industrial Revolution in this country more than any other single force.*[30]

Perhaps no industry benefited more from the railroads than the telegraph industry. American inventor Samuel Morse had unveiled the telegraph in the mid-1830s, and by the early 1850s, telegraph wires were being strung up across America.

"It is hard to imagine today, when satellites and undersea cables keep every part of the globe in instant communication with every other part, just how slowly news spread in the eighteenth century," explained one historian.

> *The battles of Lexington and Concord, the opening events of the American Revolution, occurred on Wednesday, April 19, 1775. But news of the events reached New York only on Sunday, April 23, and Philadelphia on April 24 ... And it was on May 28, fully five and a half weeks later, that the British cabinet in London learned, to its horror, that the long-smoldering crisis in*

The telegraph, shown here, which was created by Samuel Morse, changed the way people communicated with each other.

America had flashed into open war.[31]

The telegraph system gave Americans and people around the world the power to communicate instantaneously across hundreds or even thousands of miles. The first telegraph lines were strung up between eastern cities, but by the 1860s, they were following railroad lines out into the western frontier to the great benefit of both industries. Telegraph companies used existing railroad corridors to build thousands of miles of telegraph wire at a fraction of the cost that would have been involved if they had to clear land themselves. In return, railroad companies were able to use telegraphs to dispatch trains, adjust business schedules, and modernize western towns and communities that provided freight for the railroads.

These sorts of strategic alliances across industries became so commonplace that they became a standard feature of American business. Resourceful entrepreneurs and executives used such alliances to build enormous corporations and trusts that had great control over the marketplace. By the close of the 19th century, however, these corporate giants wielded so much power—and used it so ruthlessly—that the American public rebelled. As the 20th century began, this rebellion brought major changes to the still-evolving Industrial Revolution.

Chapter Four

CHANGED BY INDUSTRY

Almost every part of American life was transformed by the Industrial Revolution. Technological innovations, such as the railroad and telegraph, and economic developments, such as the rise of the factory system and corporations, provided the foundation for modern life that Americans know today. Some of the social changes that accompanied industrialization, however, were negative. Soaring rates of urban poverty and rising tensions between employers and workers are just two examples. The Age of Industrialization did, however, encourage a sustained wave of immigration to America, sparked Americans' support for public education, prompted positive change in women's rights, and gave some Americans more free time and comfortable surroundings. Whether positive or negative, the Industrial Revolution dramatically changed the American way of life.

European Immigrants and the Industrial Revolution

One key to America's rapid industrialization and settlement of the West was the massive, sustained immigration of Europeans during the 19th century. This wave of immigration stemmed in part from problems in Europe, where political turmoil, lack of economic opportunity, and crop failures afflicted many regions. European immigrants made the long and difficult journey across the Atlantic Ocean in a mood of optimism and hope. They knew that factory jobs and inexpensive land for farming awaited them in America. To these struggling men and women, the United States represented a fresh start.

By 1860, nearly one-third of men living in the northern United States had been born outside the country. As the 19th century went on, the flood of immigrants did not slow. Instead, the origins of European immigration merely shifted from

Immigrants came to America in search of a better life. They arrived in huge numbers, generally by boat, as shown here.

Germany, England, and other western European nations to Italy, Poland, and other parts of eastern Europe.

Whatever their country of origin, these European immigrants—as well as smaller numbers of immigrants from other places, including Mexico, China, and the West Indies—became essential to America's stunning economic growth. Many filled factories, steel mills, shipyards, coal mines, and oil fields, where they operated great industrial machines that rattled and roared around the clock. Some immigrants and their families lived hundreds of miles from the nearest city, but they contributed to the industrial age as well. After all, it was their labor that provided the food, coal, iron ore, and other resources that kept the cities humming. Many of these immigrants staked their futures on the Great Lakes region or the territories of the Great Plains, where they established farms or joined logging and mining companies. The immigrants who settled in rural areas of the central United States and the Great Plains faced many challenges. Some obstacles, such as weather-related crop failures and high railroad freight charges, were present throughout the rural regions. Others were unique to certain areas. In various parts of the West, for example, settlers, miners, and ranchers entered into violent conflict with Native Americans desperate to stop the white invaders from taking their lands and destroying their ways of life.

Nonetheless, many immigrant families who settled in America's cities would have gladly changed places with their rural counterparts. Working-class people in New York, Chicago, and other major cities lived in troubled surroundings. American cities grew so quickly that governments were overwhelmed. Poverty, disease, and crime filled the streets of many crowded urban neighborhoods. Millions of young children were forced by economic circumstances to work next to their parents in factories and mills.

Many immigrants tried to shield themselves from some of these problems by gathering in ethnic enclaves. In these neighborhoods, people could take comfort in their native languages and customs. These settlement patterns, though, cultivated mistrust and prejudice between isolated ethnic groups who often competed for jobs and housing.

Workers Fight for Change

As industrialization swept across America, immigrant and native-born workers alike expressed anger and frustration with their corporate employers. Most industries expected long hours of hard work from their unskilled and semiskilled workers. Extremely long workweeks—60 or 70 hours—were common, and many jobs took a significant physical toll. Workers were almost always paid poorly, and they often endured hazardous working conditions. In fact, employers had no legal responsibility for injuries or deaths suffered in their factories, and few owners felt any moral obligation to keep their employees safe. Around the turn of the 20th century, roughly 30,000 industrial workers were killed annually, and another 1 million suffered injury. "By present standards the age of America's first Industrial Revolution must be regarded as callous in its relative indifference to the welfare and safety of workers," described one historian. "The unemployed worker was cast adrift. As a rule, there was no such thing as public relief, and private charity was either insufficient or offered only on demeaning terms. The risks of injury or death on the job were grievously high."[32]

American workers tried to change working conditions by joining together in labor unions. These unions bargained with employers on behalf of their members on a range of issues. They sought better wages and benefits, shorter work hours, more flexible work rules, and safer working conditions. In the post–Civil War era, some unions of skilled craftsmen did manage to negotiate significant wage and workplace improvements for their

George Meany, who was the leader of the American Federation of Labor-Congress of Industrial Organizations (AFL-CIO), worked hard to ensure that workers got the rights they deserved.

Upton Sinclair and His Muckraking Fame

The famous American journalist Upton Beall Sinclair was born on September 20, 1878, in Baltimore. He set out to make a career for himself as a writer and investigative reporter at an early age. Sinclair did not achieve fame, though, until he published *The Jungle* in 1906. This novel painted such a grim—and accurate—picture of the horrible conditions in the U.S. meatpacking industry that the American public demanded reforms. The U.S. Congress and President Theodore Roosevelt responded by passing the Pure Food and Drug Act and the Meat Inspection Act in 1906.

The uproar over *The Jungle* established Sinclair as the most prominent of America's muckrakers, a term mockingly applied to a group of turn-of-the-century journalists who used their writing to expose political corruption, social problems, and corporate trickery. As the years passed, Sinclair wrote dozens of novels, essays, and investigative reports. Many of these works reflected the author's commitment to social justice and his strong belief in socialism.

In the 1920s, Sinclair's political activism led him to make two unsuccessful bids for Congress. In 1934, he won the Democratic nomination for California's governorship with a platform he called EPIC (End Poverty in California), but he was defeated by Republican nominee Frank Merriam in the general election. Sinclair returned to writing, and in 1943, he received the Pulitzer Prize for his novel *Dragon's Teeth*. Sinclair died November 25, 1968.

members. However, unskilled and semiskilled workers did not have the same bargaining power. Their efforts to improve their circumstances and better provide for their families were typically crushed by corporate owners determined to maximize their profits. Sometimes, big mining, railroad, and manufacturing companies with political influence even called in National Guard troops or local police to break strikes and harass union leaders. The ruthless strategies of America's corporate giants made it hard for unions to make significant gains, and union membership remained low—further hurting their bargaining power.

Despite disappointments, activists such as Samuel Gompers of the American Federation of Labor (AFL), John Mitchell of the United Mine Workers of America (UMWA), labor leader Mary Harris "Mother" Jones, populist politician

Upton Sinclair is shown here shaking hands with President Lyndon Johnson at a 1967 ceremony after Johnson passed a new meat inspection law.

William Jennings Bryan, and Socialist Eugene Debs continued to fight for workers' rights in the late 1800s and early 1900s. Their calls for economic and social justice were echoed by journalists—sometimes called muckrakers—such as Upton Sinclair, Ida Tarbell, and Jacob Riis. The stories published by these investigative reporters detailed crushing poverty in slums, brutal working conditions in factories, and ways in which big business manipulated the nation's political, judicial, and economic systems.

A New Century

By the dawn of the 20th century, public calls for business and social reform were impossible to ignore. Many middle-class people had joined working-class critics in concluding that the wealthy industrialists who directed the country's huge corporations and trusts were more concerned with economic and political power than the well-being of their fellow citizens. These Americans welcomed the economic growth and excitement that industrialization had brought, but they worried that big business bore a heavy responsibility for the poverty and political corruption that troubled the nation. "The rise of large-scale corporations was unsettling, even frightening," wrote one scholar.

> *United States Steel, Standard Oil, and the rest were certainly remarkable creations [and] they provided a host of new goods and services, often at lower costs ... [But] they wielded disturbing economic power: more than one industry had become an oligopoly, basically controlled by a handful of large firms. The corporations could hurt consumers by raising the price of goods; they could hurt farmers and businessmen by raising railroad rates and hiking the cost of raw materials; they could hurt workers by cutting wages and demanding more productivity; they could hurt competitors by slashing the price of finished products and raising the price of raw materials; they could hurt towns, cities, whole regions of the country by manipulating freight charges and putting railroads and factories in one locale or another.*[33]

This unhappiness with the direction of American society became so profound that political leaders finally responded. They passed laws designed to diminish the power of the corporate giants and address social problems created by industrialization. "The captains of industry who have driven the railway systems across this continent, who have built up our commerce, who have developed our manufactures, have on the whole done great good to our people," President Theodore Roosevelt admitted in 1903. "Yet it is also true that there are real and grave evils [in corporate America] ... and a resolute and practical effort must be made to correct these evils."[34]

From the 1890s through 1920, numerous laws were passed at the city, state, and federal levels to reduce the influence of big business and increase the rights of workers. Some of these laws were ineffective, but others did reduce exploitation of workers, help the elderly, decrease the use of child labor, and eliminate business monopolies in certain industries. All of this legislation ushered in a new chapter in American history: From this point forward, the U.S. government would take a much more active role in regulating business activity and addressing social problems.

Girl Power

The Industrial Revolution triggered major changes in the lives of women. Prior to industrialization, men and women carried out the work necessary to thrive in America's farming-oriented economy. Most chores and duties were divided based on gender. Men had greater responsibility for fieldwork, while women spent more of their time tending to housework and raising children. Nonetheless, husbands and wives generally worked as a team to make their farms successful, and they often spent time with each other over the course of a day.

As the Industrial Revolution swept across the United States, this changed. Large numbers of families left rural America for the fast-growing cities. Once they settled in cities, men took factory jobs, and women were left to take care of the children and numerous household chores associated with 19th-century life. Some young women entered the industrial world as well—most visibly in the New England textile mills—but they generally were segregated from male workers, and they often left these jobs once they married and started families.

By the mid-19th century, industrialization had expanded the need for clerks, managers, engineers, and skilled craftsmen, all of whom became members of the nation's ever-growing middle class. Men almost always filled these positions, leaving their wives with more leisure time, yet women's opportunities for personal growth were, in some ways, more limited than ever before. The men who dominated industrialized society came to view the home as a relaxing break from the factory floors and corporate offices in which they worked. They made it clear that they wanted their wives and daughters to devote their energies and talents to the home and leave the messy arenas of business and politics to men. In this culture, the most highly prized women were those who displayed good manners, high morals, and quiet obedience to husbands and fathers.

Some women, though, openly rebelled at these restrictions. They wanted to end their exclusion from the exciting new business world that industrialization had created. They also wanted increased access to higher education and greater freedom to make their own life choices and their own judgments about "moral" and "appropriate" behavior. Finally, they wanted more of a voice in politics. They knew if they had suffrage—the right to vote—issues that were important to them would get attention.

All of these factors contributed to campaigns for suffrage and women's rights in the second half of the 19th century. The birth of the women's rights movement in America is often traced to an 1848 convention at Seneca Falls, New York, that was organized by Lucretia Mott and Elizabeth Cady Stanton. At first, people made fun of the movement or simply ignored it. Time and time again, however, activists successfully framed the issue of suffrage as one of basic justice. "It was we, the people," famous suffragist Susan B. Anthony argued. "Not we, the white male citizens; nor yet we, the male citizens; but we, the whole people, who formed the Union. And we formed it, not to give the blessings of liberty, but to secure them; not to the half of ourselves and the half of our posterity, but to the whole people—women as well as men."[35]

Public support for suffrage and women's rights strengthened throughout the last decades of the 19th century. The

Women were an important part of the work force, and they called for changes that would help them support their families.

battle continued into the early 20th century under a new generation of leaders, such as Alice Paul and Carrie Chapman Catt. On August 26, 1920, the right to vote was finally extended to American women when the 19th Amendment became part of the U.S. Constitution.

Public Education: Teaching the Masses

The Industrial Revolution had a significant impact on the American education system. Prior to the 1830s, a national public school system did not exist in the United States. Formal schooling was not even available in some parts of the

Alice Paul: Campaigning for Justice

Alice Paul was born January 11, 1885, in Mt. Laurel, New Jersey. As Paul grew up, her Quaker parents instilled in her a strong sense of social justice and a deep belief in women's suffrage. After earning a doctoral degree from the University of Pennsylvania in 1912, Paul began advocating for expanded women's rights in America—and she was not afraid to fight. She supported aggressive political and social tactics to achieve greater gender equality.

Drawing other like-minded women to the cause, she quickly established herself as one of the nation's most outspoken champions of women's voting rights. Paul helped found the National Woman's Party in 1917. This organization quickly became well known for its confrontational tactics and passionate membership. Paul organized hunger strikes and protests in front of the White House. She was arrested and jailed on several occasions for these activities, but historians believe that her activism and hard work helped convince President Woodrow Wilson to publicly support women's voting rights in 1918.

In 1920, the 19th Amendment to the Constitution, which gave American women the right to vote, was ratified and became law. With this victory under her belt, Paul moved on to become a leading women's rights advocate on other issues. She also became a prominent peace activist in the 1930s and 1940s. Paul died on July 9, 1977.

country, and children of wealthy families received far greater levels of instruction (often from private tutors) than did children from poor, working-class, or even middle-class backgrounds.

In the 1830s and 1840s, New England reformers began calling for the establishment of free public schools across the country. Despite the fact that these schools would be paid for through higher taxes, major manufacturing companies were among the most enthusiastic supporters. Their influence with lawmakers made passage of laws supporting public schools more likely. "Enlightened self-interest, another name for corporate social responsibility, guided [the corporations]," one historian explained. Businessmen realized that "a literate and numerate work force would be more productive than an ignorant one ... The school would [teach] habits of punctuality, self-discipline, and obedience to authority."[36]

In 1852, Massachusetts passed the

nation's first mandatory school attendance laws. Many other states quickly followed, although it was not until 1918 that all states had such laws in place. During the second half of the 19th century, state legislatures also moved to provide funding for public schools for all American children. By the end of the 19th century, free elementary public school systems were in place in every state. In 1925, though, Catholic opposition to public schooling led to a U.S. Supreme Court ruling that permitted parents to enroll children in private schools. This mix of public and private elementary and high school systems remains in place today.

One unexpected change following the Industrial Revolution was the spread of public education. Most of America's children learned in small schoolhouses similar to this one.

Daily Life in America

Other familiar parts of daily life in the United States began to take shape across America during the 19th century. Just like so many other aspects of existence in that century, the Industrial Revolution played an important role in that transformation.

For example, industrialization transformed the infrastructure of American society. Sewer systems, gaslight-illuminated streets, public transit systems (in the form of streetcars), skyscrapers, luxury liners, and sophisticated waterworks all became realities during this era. In addition, technology made homes more comfortable. By the 1850s, for example, many homes of the wealthy and middle class were outfitted with central heating and gaslight fixtures.

Advances in communication and transportation, meanwhile, opened new worlds of opportunity, recreation, and adventure for Americans. "Before the early nineteenth century ... people seldom ventured more than fifty miles from where they had been born, or, if they did, never saw their birthplace again," one historian observed.

> *Now, in less than a lifetime, it had become possible to travel a hundred miles in a day, receive instant word from someone a thousand miles away, and read of events that were taking place, right then, halfway around the world. It was possible to have hot water run out of a tap, be warm on the coldest night, read a book at night without eyestrain.*
>
> *These miracles of daily life that piled one upon the other in the first decades of the nineteenth century ... induced a mood of optimism and a belief in progress that had not been known before.*[37]

The industrialization of the United States created an increasingly consumer-oriented society. Many Americans did not have the economic resources to take part in this transition, but those who did have the money rushed to purchase the wide array of products available. They bought processed foods, decorative furniture, household cleaning products, toys and games, ready-made clothing for work and play, and countless other goods that had not existed in large quantities just a few years earlier. By the 1890s, big department stores and other mass retail outlets were seen across the country. Many famous names in retail business history, such as Woolworths, Macy's, Marshall Field's, and Sears, emerged during this period. Easy access to these goods made life more convenient, and people welcomed the change.

Bicycles and other sports equipment were popular with consumers in the final decades of the 19th century. Their popularity reflected the nation's growing interest in leisure and recreational activities. Musicals, stage shows, circuses, and other forms of

A Sports Celebrity

John L. Sullivan was the last and most famous of the prizefighting champions in boxing's pre-glove era. Born in Roxbury, Massachusetts, on October 15, 1858, Sullivan entered the world of prizefighting in his teens. By the late 1870s, he was known in many parts of the country for his fist-fighting skills.

No formal boxing titles existed in Sullivan's time, but historians agree that he was the foremost heavyweight boxer in America—and possibly the world—from the early 1880s through 1892, when he lost to "Gentleman Jim" James J. Corbett in a 21-round match. During his reign as the unofficial heavyweight champion of the world, Sullivan became a celebrity. However, newspaper coverage of the era often painted him as little more than an alcoholic troublemaker, so he was both loved and hated by boxing fans.

After losing to Corbett, Sullivan's fame quickly faded. He supported himself by touring on the vaudeville—a type of stage show—circuit, but he was virtually forgotten until 1905, when he announced that he had sworn off alcohol and become a temperance activist. He never regained his fame or wealth, but he spoke out in favor of Prohibition, or the national ban on alcohol.

John L. Sullivan is shown here fighting in a bareknucle, or pre-glove, boxing math during the late 1800s.

live entertainment drew huge audiences of paying customers, and sports such as football, basketball, racing, and wrestling caught people's interest. The public's passion for sports became so great that the most noted athletes of the era, such as boxer John L. Sullivan, were among the most famous American figures.

The rise of sports in American culture was due in large part to the increases in free time and income that came to many Americans after industrialization. The popularity of sports and recreation reflected growing American confidence in itself at century's end. Many citizens of the United States believed that their country, once a possession of faraway Britain, was rising to the top of the world powers.

Chapter Five

INVENTIONS AND INNOVATIONS IN THE 20TH CENTURY

Although the Industrial Revolution started and hit its peak in the 19th century, it entered a new and exciting phase in the early 20th century. New machines—including the telephone, automobile, and airplane—became widespread and allowed people to connect like never before. These inventions—and other advances in numerous other industries—transformed daily life for Americans. The economic development that accompanied these inventions allowed the United States to achieve economic dominance in the world.

From Telegraph to Telephone

One invention that changed business and culture in the 20th century—the telephone—had actually been introduced in the 1870s. However, Alexander Graham Bell's invention did not replace the telegraph as the nation's leading communication tool until the early 1900s.

In its earliest decades, the telephone industry was dominated by the Bell Telephone Company and its long-distance service company, American Telephone & Telegraph (AT&T). This near-monopoly was brief, though. Bell remained the industry's giant, but by 1900, smaller companies were supplying service to more than 1 million telephone owners across the country. The independent companies could not compete with Bell in the big cities, but they prospered in more rural areas of the country.

These smaller firms were able to survive because of steadily rising demand for the telephone. Indeed, Bell's invention swept across the country with amazing speed. Between 1910 and 1930, telephone ownership skyrocketed from 7.5 million to well over

The invention of the telephone helped to create jobs because operators were needed to connect calls.

20 million. After all, the benefits of the telephone were clear to nearly everyone. It greatly aided business enterprises and government agencies, and it enabled people to talk to friends and family who lived far away. The telephone was particularly treasured in rural communities because it helped ward off feelings of isolation and loneliness that haunted many farming families.

The telephone was not universally loved. A few observers expressed concern that the telephone—along with other innovations such as the streetcar and automobile—were eroding traditional community ties. Most of these critics were from an older, more conservative generation. They believed the traditional American way of life, including an agricultural economy and tight family ties, was the only way to head toward the future.

These concerns were drowned out by the enthusiasm that most felt for the new device. During the 1920s and 1930s, the telephone industry continued to grow, defying the economic downturn of the Great Depression. During this time, AT&T (which had become the parent company to Bell in 1899) reestablished its monopoly over the industry, and it became more advanced and widespread with every passing year. By 1940, the company had not only established phone service to most American homes and businesses, it had also opened international service. "From World War I to 1940," wrote one historian, "competition almost ceased as the companies divided the telephone business among themselves under the [control] of AT&T and the supervision of federal and state regulators. The telephone system remained essentially the same as it was on the eve of World War II until … AT&T [broke up] forty-four years later."[38]

Radio and Wireless Broadcast

Wireless broadcast radio was another major milestone of the Industrial Revolution. This breakthrough in communications technology gave American business an exciting new avenue through which it could advertise its products and services. It also brought in a new era in popular entertainment and became a centerpiece of family life throughout the first half of the 20th century.

Late–19th century inventors and scientists, such as Guglielmo Marconi and Nikola Tesla, were among the first to experiment with harnessing radio waves for long-distance communication. During the 1900s and 1910s, European and American engineers and entrepreneurs built on their work, refining the technology and experimenting with ways to harness radio's possibilities for profit. It was not until the early 1920s that commercial radio broadcasting became a reality. In 1920, KDKA, a station based in Pittsburgh, became the first government-licensed commercial radio broadcasting station in the United States. Over the next few years, hundreds more stations scrambled to get recognized and receive their licenses.

The 1920s were years of general economic prosperity and optimism in the United States, and many Americans came to view radio—along with the automobile—as one of the

KDKA's first radio broadcast in 1920 sparked a trend in news, commerce, and entertainment that would last for decades.

strongest symbols of this miraculous new age. American families loved the fact that they could now hear live musical performances, sporting events, comedy shows, news headlines, and all sorts of other entertainment in their living rooms with the turn of a dial, and they rushed to purchase radio sets and equipment from local stores. In 1925 alone, reports estimate that 2 million radio sets were sold in America. By 1926, one-sixth of all homes had a radio set. As historians have noted, the new technology quickly replaced newspapers as the country's preferred source of news and entertainment:

> *The prosperity and brashness of the Roaring Twenties, including the increasing domination of big business over the economy, gave importance to radio's live, national advertising potential ... By and large it was a time of [wealth] and material possessions, the growth of a new economic middle class, new opportunities through mass production for unskilled and skilled workers, and a national ... euphoria. Radio fit perfectly into this heady postwar world, sometimes informing, sometimes educating, sometimes assuaging, and mostly entertaining.*[39]

The leading radio broadcasters of this era were the Columbia Broadcasting System (CBS) and the National Broadcasting Company (NBC), both of which developed impressive national networks of local radio stations. These networks became even more valuable after passage of the Radio Act of 1927. This act created the Federal Radio Commission (FRC) to oversee and regulate all aspects of broadcasting. For NBC, CBS, and other industry participants, however, the most important duty of the FRC was to assign specific radio frequencies to individual stations. This change brought much-needed order to the airwaves. The number of radio stations had grown so quickly that the entire industry had been in danger of smothering itself in a huge storm of competing radio signals.

As it turned out, broadcast radio's position as America's leading source of news and entertainment would be short-lived. Radio continues to exist, of course, as a popular source of music, entertainment, and news, and millions still listen to commercial or satellite radio daily. In the 1950s, however, a new communications medium called television arrived, and American business and society were changed forever.

The Television Takeover

The earliest television technology grew out of the work of numerous inventors, scientists, and engineers at the beginning of the 20th century, but the first working electronic television systems did not appear until the 1920s. At that time, the CBS and NBC radio networks took the lead in pursuing commercial applications for this dawning technology. Several executives and inventors provided important contributions to television technology during this time, including Philo Farnsworth and Vladimir Zworykin.

Perhaps no one was as important to the industry's development as David Sarnoff, who headed the Radio Corporation of America (RCA)—the parent company of NBC. Sarnoff was convinced that television was the world's next great leap in communication, and he worked tirelessly to see his vision become a reality. "[Television] is a new art so important in its implications that it is bound to affect all society," he declared in 1939. "It is an art which shines like a torch of hope in the troubled world ... This miracle of engineering skill which one day will bring the world to the home also brings a new American industry to serve man's material welfare. [It] will become an important factor in American economic life."[40]

In the 1930s, RCA, CBS, and NBC began experimenting with commercial television broadcasts. These early efforts were largely ignored. The Great Depression seriously dampened public interest in the new technology, and World War II brought almost all television manufacturing and broadcasting activity to a halt. After the war, American households found themselves riding a wave of major economic prosperity. Armed with well-paying jobs—and eager to put memories of the Depression and war behind them—families rushed to buy televisions. Television ownership, which was just 10 percent of American homes in 1950, rose to 87 percent by 1960. The introduction of color television sets gave another big boost to television's popularity, and by the early 1970s, a large portion of the nation's sets were color.

In 1961, government official Newton J. Minow delivered a famous speech that accused television broadcasters of creating a form of entertainment that emphasized mindless viewing, not programming that could create informed and responsible citizens. More than three decades later, Minow insisted that little had changed:

> *Every day, all across the United States, a parade of louts, losers, and con men whom most people would never allow in their homes enter anyway, through television. And every day the strangers spend more time with America's children than teachers do, or even in many cases the parents themselves ... No other major democratic nation in the world has so willingly turned its children over to ... strangers this way. No other democratic nation has so willingly converted its children into markets for commercial gain and ignored their moral, intellectual, and social development.*[41]

Today, decades after it first burst onto the cultural scene, television remains an influential presence in the lives of nearly

David Sarnoff is remembered as one of the biggest names in the early history of television. His beliefs about the power of the technology were amazingly accurate.

The Big Three

Today, television features an overwhelming number of cable and satellite network channels, as well as subscription-based networks with no commercials. From the 1950s through the 1970s, however, virtually all television programming came from three networks of allied local stations. These networks—CBS, NBC, and ABC—all began as radio networks. CBS was formed in 1927 through the merger of United Independent Broadcasters, which was a radio broadcasting company, and the Columbia Phonograph Company. NBC had been launched one year earlier by RCA, which was one of the nation's largest radio manufacturers. NBC was the industry leader for more than 15 years. It grew so large, in fact, that it divided itself into two radio networks, called Red and Blue. In 1943, concerns about NBC's growing monopoly led the U.S. government to force NBC to sell off its Blue network. This network became the basis for the American Broadcasting Company (ABC).

Thanks to years of operation in the radio industry, the Big Three had the best communication technology, news organizations, and entertainers when television became popular in the 1950s. Armed with these assets, they easily took control of U.S. television. Public television stations and a small number of independent stations operated as well, but neither had the financial resources to compete with the big networks. As a result, the Big Three divided up virtually all American viewers until the 1970s, when improved technology enabled new cable television stations to emerge on the scene.

all Americans. It remains a major source of information and entertainment and has long ranked as the business world's leading medium for marketing products and services to consumers. However, some worry that television programming has done long-lasting damage to American culture and society. These critics acknowledge that some television programs are educational and worthwhile, but they argue that much of the content broadcast into homes glorifies inappropriate behavior, such as violence or drug use.

The Automobile Industry

The third major innovation that transformed American business and society in the early 20th century was the automobile. This industry came out of Detroit, Michigan, in the opening years of the century. By the 1910s, it was clear that this invention was becoming an important part American life. From

The Model T, shown here, remains one of the most iconic symbols of the 20th century. Automobiles revolutionized travel across the world.

1900 to 1910 alone, the total number of cars produced in the United States rose dramatically—from 4,000 to 187,000.

Automobiles were created during this period by hundreds of small companies. The single most influential automobile in America, though, was the Model T, which was introduced by Henry Ford in 1908. Reliable and affordable, the Model T ushered in the Age of the Automobile. By 1920, Ford's vehicles accounted for 60 percent of the motor vehicles in the country. This was possible because of Ford's assembly line system of production. In this relatively new form of organizing employees, each worker was responsible for just one component of the car, and when they finished their section, the product was sent on to the next person in the assembly line.

This stunning success made Ford one of the most admired individuals in the history of American business. "Opinion polls in the 1920s ranked Henry Ford just behind Jesus and Napoleon in the public's estimation of the greatest men in history," one historian noted. "Ford was the embodiment of enterprise, vision, and mechanical invention … More than any other inventor, more than any artist, writer, or politician, Henry Ford made American dreams come true."[42]

The rapid spread of the automobile was greatly aided by the introduction of credit purchasing plans. Throughout

Henry Ford's assembly lines allowed cars to be produced faster. Each worker was responsible for a specific part of the process of building an automobile.

Henry Ford

Famed automaker Henry Ford was born in Michigan in 1863. He studied and worked to be an engineer, and in the early 1890s, he took a job with Thomas Edison's Detroit Illuminating Company. During this time, Ford began experimenting with automobile designs, and by the end of the century, he had built several working prototypes. These successes attracted the attention of investors, and in 1903, he launched the Ford Motor Company.

In 1908, Ford unveiled a new automobile, the Model T, which ranks as the most famous and influential automobile in the history of the industry. Ford was able to sell the reliable Model T at a price that attracted middle-class buyers because his introduction of the assembly line kept production costs low. Ford's assembly line was quickly adopted by other industries, and it remains a feature of modern industrial manufacturing.

Ford built an automotive empire during the 1910s and 1920s, and his 1914 decision to pay his workers a very high wage for the era further boosted his reputation as one of America's finest citizens. He was a generous donor who established hospitals and charitable foundations that exist well into the 21st century. As time passed, his reputation as a hero of the industrial age was tarnished by his prejudicial views against Jewish people, his controlling attitude toward his workforce, and his ruthless attempts to stifle labor unions. In 1945, Ford turned over the reins of the company to his grandson, Henry Ford II, and retired. He died at his Dearborn, Michigan, estate in 1947.

most of American history, if someone wanted something, they most likely paid for it with cash—in full. Purchasing something on credit was almost the exact opposite of this. If someone wanted to buy a car, for example, they would make a down payment with their dealer (typically 10 or 20 percent of the price) and promise to pay off the rest over time. These plans enabled Americans to buy the newest appliances, including refrigerators, vacuum cleaners, radios, hair dryers, and other goods powered by electricity. Because more businesses were willing to sell on credit, the appliance industry boomed. Credit plans were also important to the growth of the automobile industry, since the purchase of an automobile—from the cheapest to the most luxurious—carried a considerable price tag that few American families could pay in cash.

By the end of the 1920s, motor vehicles had spread to all corners of the United States. By 1929, there were approximately 27 million vehicles on American roads. This growth not only reflected enthusiasm for the freedom these cars provided, but also the rising importance of car and truck transportation to other industries.

The high demand for automobiles encouraged the industry to make its operations more efficient and profitable. Alfred Sloan's reorganization of the administration of General Motors in the 1920s was particularly momentous for American business and industry. Sloan changed the company from a loose collection of associated companies, with blurred lines of accountability and supervision, into divisions that had power to quickly respond to changing market conditions and that had to operate within policies set out by a powerful board of managers. He also introduced successful new marketing strategies, such as small changes in the appearance of automobile models from year to year. These cosmetic changes cost General Motors relatively little money, but they attracted millions of customers who wanted to make sure that they had the most recent model. Sloan's revolution in company management not only vaulted General Motors to the top of the industry in the 1930s, it also changed how other industries organized their operations.

A Massive Industry

Meanwhile, the automobile industry provided a new market for other industries. By the end of the 1920s, carmakers were consuming about 10 percent of the nation's wood, 15 percent of its iron and steel, and 25 percent of its aluminum. The industry also prompted new waves of road and highway construction, commercial development, and residential housing construction across the country. Finally, automobile owners needed gasoline to run their machines, so they became a leading source of income for oil producers.

The Great Depression of the 1930s took a heavy toll on automakers. However, the demand for planes, tanks, clothing, food, and other goods during World War II got factories roaring again. When the United States emerged from the war in 1945, it entered a period of economic prosperity that lasted through the 1950s. Ford Motor Company, General Motors, and the Chrysler Corporation—the so-called Big Three of U.S. automakers—reaped the benefits of the rising economy. In the decade after World War II, the number of passenger cars on American roads shot up to nearly 50 million. The profits of oil companies jumped as well, as gasoline consumption soared.

The midcentury growth of America's oil companies provided a clear example of the importance of the auto industry to the nation's economic health.

When automakers suffered declines in sales, the ripples were felt in other industries; when auto makers thrived, the entire economy benefited. "If any industry represented America's industrial might in the 20th century, surely it was auto makers," one historian wrote. "The handful of companies clustered around Detroit produced the assembly line in 1913, tanks and aircraft engines during World War II, and thousands of high-paying factory jobs when peace came. The industry became the backbone of the U.S. economy and its companies America's bellwethers. As cars went, so went the nation."[43]

The Flight of a New Industry

The last chapter in the Industrial Revolution's impact on transportation was written by the inventors and entrepreneurs who made air travel a reality. For centuries, people across the globe had dreamed of finding a way to take flight, but it was not until December 17, 1903, that this dream came true. On that day, brothers Orville and Wilbur Wright's motor-powered glider was airborne for a 12-second flight covering 120 feet (36.6 m) near Kitty Hawk, North Carolina.

Surprisingly, this did not attract a great deal of public attention when it occurred. Over the next few years, the Wright brothers and American and European inventors made a flurry of technological advances, but government and industry remained disinterested until World War I. At that time, European aircraft came to play such an important role in the conflict that U.S. officials and investors finally took a serious look at the airplane. During and after the war, America began to invest much more heavily in the industry. The U.S. Post Office introduced airmail service between Washington, D.C., and New York in 1918, and the military began acquiring airplanes in increasing numbers. This market gave a much-needed boost to early American aircraft makers.

The commercial potential of airplanes, meanwhile, became evident in May 1927, when American aviator Charles Lindbergh completed a nonstop flight from New York to Paris, France, over the course of two days. This feat made Lindbergh an international hero and convinced investors and ordinary Americans that long-distance flight could one day be a safe way to travel. It also gave momentum to governmental efforts to implement rules and regulations for the fast-growing industry. By the end of the 1920s, airplanes and pilots were subject to a number of licensing and operating regulations. In addition, the U.S. government passed laws that enabled private carriers to deliver mail. This became an important source of income for America's first generation of air carriers.

In the 1930s, U.S. and European aircraft continued to get bigger, stronger, and faster. Advances in engine and propeller design, landing gear, navigation instruments, and wing design made airplanes more efficient. This proved essential during World War II, when American air power helped the Allies defeat the Axis Powers. By the time the war ended in 1945, jet-powered engines were ready for use not only in military aircraft, but also for business and travel.

During the 1950s and 1960s, advances in aeronautics came so quickly that technological marvels seemed

Wilbur Wright is shown here operating the controls of the flying machine he invented with his brother, Orville.

Flight: The Wright Idea

Aviation pioneers Orville and Wilbur Wright were born into a Midwestern farming family in post–Civil War America. Wilbur was born on April 16, 1867, in Millville, Indiana, and Orville was born on August 19, 1871, in Dayton, Ohio. In 1892, the brothers opened a bicycle shop in Dayton, and over the next few years, they began manufacturing bikes for sale. During this same period, they began following the progress of European inventors who were experimenting with gliders as a vehicle for manned flight. They even struck up a friendship with French glider expert Octave Chanute, who encouraged the Wright brothers when they began conducting their own glider experiments.

From 1900 to 1902, the Wright brothers worked exhaustively on kite and glider designs. In 1903, their efforts paid off when they made the first airplane flight near Kitty Hawk. Two years later, they built an airplane that could remain airborne for more than a half hour, and in 1908, Orville made the world's first flight of over one hour at a demonstration for U.S. Army officials. That same year, Wilbur piloted dozens of flights to impress French investors.

Around this time, the Wrights became entangled in legal battles with plane manufacturers, whom they accused of violating their design patents and rights. Then, in May 1912, Wilbur died from typhoid fever. Orville gave up flying a few years later. He spent the rest of his life as a flight researcher and designer of aeronautical equipment. He died of a heart attack on January 30, 1948. Both brothers are world-famous for their innovations.

to appear with each passing month. Supersonic flights, guided missiles, space satellites, and manned rockets designed for space exploration all burst out of the world of science fiction to become realities. Much of the investment and research that made these marvels possible came from the ongoing Cold War, a four-decade-long economic and military rivalry between the United States and the Soviet Union that began immediately after World War II. During this era, commercial air travel grew by leaps and bounds. By the mid-1970s, thousands of airports across America offered hundreds of thousands of flights to and from major eastern cities, rural western towns, and everywhere in between.

America's Economy of Consumers

The manufacturers and carriers of the commercial air travel industry were successful for the same reason that other U.S. manufacturers and retail businesses thrived: Steady industrial and economic expansion had transformed the people of the United States into the greatest consumers of goods and services on the planet. The broad outlines of this modern consumer economy had become visible as early as the Roaring Twenties. However, the massive consumer economy did not truly arrive until the 1950s and 1960s. In these decades—which were marked by the introduction of shopping malls, credit cards, and other familiar elements of modern consumerism—America became a nation of shoppers.

After World War II, the surging economic power of the United States became obvious to everyone. As business magazine *Fortune* declared in June 1953,

> *All history can show no more [amazing] economic phenomenon than today's American market. It is colossal, soaking up half the world's steel and oil, and three-fourths of its cars and appliances. The whole world fears it and is baffled by it. Let U.S. industry slip 5 percent, and waves of [fear] sweep through foreign [leaders]. Let U.S. consumer spending lag even half as much, and the most eminent economists anxiously read the omens. The whole world also marvels at and envies this market. It is enabling Americans to raise their standard of living every year while other countries have trouble in maintaining theirs. And of course the whole world wants to get in on it. For it still can punish the incompetent and inefficient, and still reward handsomely the skillful, efficient, and daring.*[44]

This sustained economic boom was driven by many factors—not a single event or invention. Increased access to government loans, expanded credit, longer shopping hours, new housing and other development associated with suburbanization, and the introduction of shopping malls all contributed to what some critics have called "affluenza"—excessive consumer consumption. As one historical commentator has noted, "Perhaps no single cause was as responsible for the emerging postwar epidemic of affluenza than the … box that found its way into most American homes by the 1950s."[45] This box—television—became the primary means by which American industry marketed goods and services to consumers. It helped create a powerful appetite for everything from automobiles to appliances to beauty products. By 1970, Americans were spending four times as much shopping as Europeans.

Some critics have said U.S. consumer spending has gotten out of control.

They believe Americans have become excessively materialistic and that their heavy levels of consumption have become a threat to the planet's limited natural resources. They also claim that Americans spend so much on unnecessary goods and services that they jeopardize their own long-term economic security. Others defend U.S. spending habits, arguing that consumers should not have to apologize for providing a comfortable, enjoyable life for themselves and their families. Regardless of which side of this debate historians defend, there is no doubt that the cause is the same: the Industrial Revolution.

Epilogue

AN INDUSTRIALIZED WORLD

The modern world bears little resemblance to the world of the Industrial Revolution. However, contemporary America owes its existence to the likes of pioneers such as Robert Fulton, Henry Ford, Eli Whitney, John D. Rockefeller, and other business legends. Inventions from the 19th and early 20th centuries are still important to society. Automobiles and airplanes remain the most popular means of travel; telephones (and now smartphones) have become essential; and machine-oriented factories, refineries, and shipyards remain important centers of economic activity.

However, some U.S. industries that thrived during the Industrial Revolution are far less influential than they once were. Textile manufacturing, for example, takes place mainly in European and Asian countries, and the telegraph has been replaced by email, phones, and other forms of communication. Railroads were once the most important element in the country's quickly growing economy and expanding geography, but today, many are no longer used for passenger travel. These advances show that the U.S. economy is defined by incredibly rapid technological, political, and cultural change. The face of business and industry continues to grow, change, and adapt.

Influenced by Industry

American business at the beginning of the 21st century is different in many important ways than it was a century ago. Industrial pollution and extreme consumption of natural resources have been linked to climate change, species extinction, and other serious environmental problems. This knowledge has prompted heated debates on the best ways to balance economic growth and environmental protection. Government regulation and oversight of businesses has also increased, driven by concerns about workplace safety, fair treatment of employees, and financial security of workers who retire or get injured on the job. Industries are struggling with growing evidence that world supplies of oil—the primary fuel of the Industrial Age—are being used at a frightening rate. This prospect has led to the emergence of new industries devoted to alternative energy sources.

The American Workforce

During the first half of the 20th century, unionization of the American workforce increased at a steady rate. At the height of the Great Depression in the mid-1930s, union membership stood at only 3 million members. General economic prosperity, talented and dedicated union leadership, and the support of powerful politicians such as Franklin D. Roosevelt later boosted the fortunes of labor organizations. By 1945, 12 million American workers held union memberships, largely in manufacturing industries. In 1953, the number of union members reached nearly 17 million, about one-fourth of the total U.S. workforce. However, since 1979, when the number of union workers reached a peak of 21 million, union membership has declined significantly. By 2003, union membership had fallen to 15.8 million workers, about 11.5 percent of the U.S. workforce. In 2016, union membership set a historic low at 10.7 percent of the total workforce.

A leading factor in the decline of organized labor has been the steady shift of manufacturing jobs from American soil to foreign countries. Advances in transportation, communication, and other technological areas have enabled multinational corporations—businesses with offices in countries around the globe—to move their factories and other operations to countries where they can pay workers much lower wages. Environmental and workplace regulations are also less strict in many of these countries. In addition, international trade agreements have made it easier for these same companies to ship foreign-made goods to the United States for sale. Finally, labor unions lost political power in many parts of the country in the 1980s, when pro-business politicians held growing influence in the White House and Congress.

These events have produced a remarkable drop in industrial manufacturing—the backbone of the Industrial Revolution—in the United States. Mid-century, manufacturing jobs accounted for 30 percent of all U.S. jobs. By 1999, this percentage had dropped to 19 percent. In 2016, just 10 percent of American jobs were in the manufacturing sector. During this period, jobs in the service industry— restaurants, retail stores, landscaping, hotels, and other businesses that provide services, rather than products, to customers—have increased. Economists point out that these occupations generally do not pay as well as the manufacturing jobs that are being sent to overseas factories.

By the 21st century, 60 percent of all manufactured products sold in the United States were produced overseas. This trend

Unionization allowed workers to strike, which is when a large group of people refuse to work until their demands are met.

is present across nearly all industries—from toy manufacturing to automobile production. Many parts that are used in cars built in the United States actually come from factories in Mexico and other countries. Among suppliers of manufacturing technology and equipment, the drop in U.S. production is even more startling. U.S. production of machine tools fell by two-thirds between 1998 and 2004. Machine tool makers in Japan, which has a much smaller population, have far surpassed their American competitors in profits and use worldwide. Analysts believe that these trends are likely to continue.

The global economy of the early 21st century has created opportunities for some industries. Transportation, communications, and other high-tech industries have benefited enormously from these changes. The most spectacular growth has come in the computer and software industries. When commercial microprocessors—tiny computers placed on silicon chips—were introduced into computers in the early 1970s, the computing power of these machines increased by leaps and

China's Industrial Revolution

Since the 1990s, China has been undergoing what some economists call the Second Industrial Revolution. During the 18th and 19th centuries, when Europe and the United States built industry-based economies, China remained a nation based on agriculture, with little manufacturing capacity. In the last years of the 20th century, however, the Communist leadership of China decided to expand and modernize its economy. Their policies, combined with a huge supply of labor and beneficial international trade agreements, have created an incredible explosion of building in the nation's cities. Factories, shopping centers, and office buildings have sprouted up across China, and huge quantities of oil, iron ore, and other raw materials for manufacturers arrive at Chinese seaports every day. This economic growth has sparked a tremendous migration of people in China—the most heavily populated country in the world—from rural areas into the industrializing cities.

These changes have made China one of the greatest economic powers in the world. Many analysts believe it has only tapped a fraction of its full commercial potential. In fact, economists believe that by the middle of the 21st century, China's economy could surpass that of the United States and become the most powerful commercial force on the planet.

bounds. In just a few years, computers became necessary for every large business enterprise. As one scholar noted,

> *The computer, like the steam engine, produced an economic revolution, and for precisely the same reason: it caused a collapse in the price of a fundamental input into the economic system, allowing that input to be applied to an infinity of tasks that previously had been too expensive or simply impossible. The steam engine brought down the price of work-doing energy; the computer brought down the price of storing, retrieving, and manipulating information.*[46]

America and the Internet

The computer and software industries owe much of their incredible growth and financial success to the Internet. This vast global communications system of interconnected computer networks was built in the 1970s and 1980s by a community of scientists and entrepreneurs, such as Tim Berners-Lee, Vinton Cerf,

Robert Taylor, and Steve Case. In many ways, these and other early contributors to the Internet were just as visionary as Henry Ford, Robert Fulton, and other legends of the Industrial Revolution. "The Internet … owed its exuberance and vigor to the spirit of entrepreneurs of all ages who can see a new, wide open, and limitless vista before them,"[47] one scholar wrote.

Since its emergence into general use in the early 1990s, the Internet has completely changed the way people conduct business, communicate, and spend their free time. The changes to American business and industry in the Internet Age have been particularly dramatic. For example, computer technology has made it easier for businesses to interact with existing customers and attract new customers. Websites give businesses the power to advertise products and services, communicate with clients, collect information about the use of their products, track inventory and shipping operations, and respond to customer feedback and changing customer tastes more quickly and efficiently.

Some U.S. industries have struggled to survive in this new information age. The recording industry, for example, has had to replace many of its old business practices to meet the demands of customers who have the capability to download digital recordings. Many record stores have been driven out of business by the changing environment. On the other hand, new digital corporations, such as Amazon and Facebook, have risen to become economic giants strictly on the basis of online sales and advertisements, and many other smaller companies have carved out profitable positions for themselves. In addition, thousands of other retail and manufacturing companies have found ways to use the Internet not only for online sales, but also to boost revenue from traditional stores, shops, and manufacturing facilities.

The Smartphone Revolution

Today, many have the Internet at their disposal at every moment of the day thanks to smartphones. People now have the ability to download applications, or apps, that provide entertainment, allow them to bank online, track diet and fitness goals, and connect with people around the world. Social media platforms—from Facebook to Twitter to Instagram—are catered to the smartphone market so people can stay connected. Companies such as Apple and Samsung market newer technologies, such as the smartwatch, that make daily life easier and more technological than just a few years ago. With all the exciting innovations this technology has to offer, many wonder if society is becoming too dependent on virtual communication. A common criticism is that people spend too much time focusing on their own devices and not enough time interacting face-to-face. Only time will tell what innovations will be available in the years to come, but they will unquestionably change Americans' lives in exciting ways.

"The Father of the Internet"

Vinton Gray Cerf was born on June 23, 1943, in New Haven, Connecticut. After graduating from Stanford University, he took a computer programming job with IBM, but in the early 1970s, he moved on to the Advanced Research Projects Agency (ARPA), a division of the U.S. Department of Defense. At that time, the agency was working on the world's first computer network. This network, called the ARPANET, is commonly described as a forerunner of the Internet.

During the 1970s, Cerf and his colleagues, including Robert Kahn, strung together a network of computers in locations across the country. In addition, they devised complex rules, or protocols, for network communication. They researched ways to connect the ARPANET to computer networks in Europe and elsewhere. These "internetworking" efforts eventually became the basis for the term "Internet."

Protocols introduced by Cerf and his fellow researchers became widely accepted in the late 1970s and early 1980s. Once computer scientists had these common rules to follow, the development of a global computer network became a much more achievable goal. Cerf remained at the forefront of these research efforts, and by the late 1980s, he was widely described as the "father" of the emerging Internet.

Since that time, Cerf has remained heavily involved in Internet issues—from areas of computing technology to governmental policy making. In 2004, he and Robert Kahn received the A.M. Turing Award in recognition of their essential role in the development of the Internet. As of 2017, he was serving as vice president of Google, and he was awarded the Presidential Medal of Freedom in 2005.

Though the Internet was created by a number of pioneering individuals, Vinton Cerf is undoubtedly one of the most important.

A Future of Industry

Technological innovations are being introduced into business and society with stunning speed. Virtually all tools used in daily life—including cars, computers, phones, cameras, televisions, household appliances, and home security systems—are linked to powerful networks that users can access from anywhere. Many of these advancements can trace their lineage back to the Age of Industrialization.

No one can know the exact forms that American business and culture will take a decade from now, let alone 50 or 100 years in the future. "We are watching something historic happen," wrote Microsoft founder Bill Gates, "and it will affect the world seismically, rocking us the same way the discovery of the scientific method, the invention of printing, and the arrival of the Industrial Age did."[48] Most experts, historians, and observers believe the digital age has already started to make monumental changes to American—and global—society. These changes are often dramatic, and there will undoubtedly be decades of innovation, similar to the time of the Industrial Revolution.

Whatever shape the world of business will take, it will still have its roots in the Industrial Revolution. Today's technologically advanced global economy would never have come about if it had not been for inventions such as the steam engine, cotton gin, and telegraph. According to one scholar,

> *The final tally of the industrial revolution has yet to be reckoned ... The analysis is not simply a historical exercise, for the process is ongoing. The most fearsome toll of the industrial revolution may still await us in the form of greater environmental degradation or new kinds of conflicts between the [poor and rich] at the industrial table. Great opportunities may also beckon as various societies become increasingly able to make adjustments to the industrial world ... The industrial revolution, caused by an unusual set of circumstances in world history, unleashed forces that have been hard to control. The one certainty is that the process has not slowed. It continues to shape world history, from the societies seeking higher industrial achievement to societies desperately striving to preserve a newly challenged industrial lead.*[49]

Notes

Introduction: A Century of Advancement

1. Peter N. Stearns, *The Industrial Revolution in World History*. Boulder, CO: Westview, 2007, p. 6.
2. Quoted in David Traxel, *Crusader Nation: The United States in Peace and the Great War: 1898–1920*. New York, NY: Vintage Books, 2006. PDF e-book.

Chapter One: The Industrial Revolution: Setting the Stage

3. Quoted in Kevin Hillstrom and Laurie Collier Hillstrom, eds., *Industrial Revolution in America: Textiles*. Santa Barbara, CA: ABC-CLIO, 2006, p. 34.
4. John Steele Gordon, *An Empire of Wealth: The Epic History of American Economic Power*. New York, NY: Harper Collins, 2004, pp. 88–89.
5. Quoted in Michael Burger, *The Shaping of Western Civilization: From Antiquity to the Present*. Toronto, ON: University of Toronto Press, 2013, p. 354.
6. Quoted in Karen Gerhardt Britton, *Bale O' Cotton: The Mechanical Art of Cotton Ginning*. College Station, TX: Texas A&M University Press, 1992, p. 13.
7. Gordon, *Empire of Wealth*, p. 82.
8. Quoted in Dale Anderson, *The Causes of the Civil War*. Milwaukee, WI: World Almanac Library, 2004, p. 12.
9. Quoted in John Warner Barber and Henry Howe, *Our Whole Country: Or, the Past and Present of the United States, Historical and Descriptive*, vol. 2. Cincinnati, OH: Henry Howe, 1861, p. 841.
10. Stephen Yafa, *Cotton: The Biography of a Revolutionary Fiber*. New York, NY: Penguin, 2005. PDF e-book.

Chapter Two: America's Transformation

11. Quoted in Peter L. Bernstein, *Wedding of the Waters: The Erie Canal and the Making of a Great Nation*. New York, NY: Norton, 2005, p. 343.
12. Quoted in Gordon, *Empire of Wealth*, p. 108.
13. Louis C. Hunter, *Steamboats on the Western Rivers: An Economic and Technological History*. Cambridge, MA: Harvard University Press, 1949, p. 75.
14. Gordon, *Empire of Wealth*, p. 141.
15. Quoted in Richard C. Wade, *The Urban Frontier: The Rise of Western Cities, 1790–1830*. Urbana, IL: University of Illinois Press, 1959, p. 70.
16. Gordon, *Empire of Wealth*, p. 137.
17. John Steele Gordon, *The Business of America: Tales from the*

Marketplace—American Enterprise from the Settling of New England to the Break Up of AT&T. New York, NY: Walker, 2001, p. 49.

18. Daniel Feller, *The Jacksonian Promise: America, 1815–1840*. Baltimore, MD: Johns Hopkins University Press, 1995, p. 24.
19. Barbara Freese, *Coal: A Human History*. New York, NY: Perseus, 2003, p. 109.
20. Gordon, *Empire of Wealth*, p. 175.

Chapter Three: The Golden Age of the Industrial Revolution

21. Quoted in Ian Carter, *Railways and Culture in Britain: The Epitome of Modernity*. Manchester, UK: Manchester University Press, 2001, p. 24.
22. Quoted in Hillstrom and Hillstrom, *The Industrial Revolution*, p. 192.
23. Quoted in Hillstrom and Hillstrom, *The Industrial Revolution*, p. 4.
24. Quoted in Hillstrom and Hillstrom, *The Industrial Revolution*, p. 17.
25. Quoted in David H. Bain, *Empire Express: Building the First Transcontinental Railroad*. New York, NY: Penguin, 1999, p. 6.
26. *Putnam's Monthly*, "Statistics and Speculations concerning the Pacific Railroad," *Putnam's Monthly*, September, 1853, p. 271.
27. Ron Chernow, *Titan: The Life of John D. Rockefeller*, Sr. New York, NY: Random House, 1998, p. 249.
28. John P. Hoerr, *And the Wolf Finally Came: The Decline of the American Steel Industry*. Pittsburgh, PA: University of Pittsburgh Press, 1988, p. 170.
29. James Howard Bridge, *The Carnegie Millions and the Men Who Made Them*. London, UK: Limpus, Baker & Co., 1903, p. 169
30. Gordon, *Empire of Wealth*, p. 149.
31. Gordon, *Empire of Wealth*, p. 153.

Chapter Four: Changed by Industry

32. Stuart Bruchey, *Enterprise: The Dynamic Economy of a Free People*. Cambridge, MA: Harvard University Press, 1990, p. 363.
33. Michael McGerr, *A Fierce Discontent: The Rise and Fall of the Progressive Movement in America*. New York, NY: Oxford University Press, 2003, pp. 151–152.
34. Theodore Roosevelt, "Theodore Roosevelt: First Annual Message, December 3rd, 1901," The American Presidency Project, accessed May 19, 2017. www.presidency.ucsb.edu/ws/?pid=29542.
35. Susan B. Anthony, "Woman's Right to the Suffrage," National Center for Public Policy Research, accessed May 19, 2017. www.nationalcenter.org/AnthonySuffrage.html.
36. Merle Curti, *The Social Ideas of American Educators*. New York, NY: Scribner's, 1935, pp. 83–84.
37. Gordon, *Empire of Wealth*, p. 166.

Chapter Five: Inventions and Innovations in the 20th Century

38. Claude S. Fischer, *America Calling: A Social History of the Telephone to 1940*. Berkeley, CA: University of California Press, 1992, p. 34.
39. Robert L. Hilliard and Michael C. Keith, *The Broadcast Century and Beyond: A Biography of American Broadcasting*. New York, NY: Focal, 2001, pp. 23–24.
40. Quoted in Marcy Carsey and Tom Werner, "Father of Broadcasting DAVID SARNOFF," *TIME*, December 7, 1998. content.time.com/time/magazine/article/0,9171,989773,00.html.
41. Newton N. Minow and Craig L. LaMay, *Abandoned in the Wasteland: Children, Television, and the First Amendment*. New York, NY: Hill and Wang, 1995, pp. 18–19.
42. Jack Beatty, "The Business of America," in *Colossus: How the Corporation Changed America*, Jack Beatty, ed. New York, NY: Crown, 2002. PDF e-book.
43. Joann Muller, Kathleen Kerwin, and David Welch, "Autos: A New Industry," Bloomberg, July 15, 2002. www.bloomberg.com/news/articles/2002-07-14/autos-a-new-industry.
44. Quoted in David M. Kennedy and Thomas Bailey, *The American Spirit: U.S. History as Seen by Contemporaries*, vol. 2. Boston, MA: Wadsworth, 2010, p. 481.
45. John De Graaf, David Wann, and Thomas H. Naylor, *Affluenza: How Overconsumption Is Killing Us—and How to Fight Back*. San Francisco, CA: Berrett-Koehler, 2014, p. 136.

Epilogue: An Industrialized World

46. Gordon, *Empire of Wealth*, p. 409.
47. Quoted in Robert Sobel, *The Great Boom 1950–2000: How a Generation of Americans Created the World's Most Prosperous Society*. New York, NY: St. Martin's, 2000. PDF e-book.
48. Bill Gates, *The Road Ahead*. New York, NY: Penguin, 1995, p. 313.
49. Stearns, *The Industrial Revolution in World History*, p. 297.

For More Information

Books

Baron, Robert C. *Pioneers and Plodders: The American Industrial Spirit*. Golden, CO: Fulcrum, 2004.
This book provides a historical overview of business leaders in four industries: steel, automobiles, electronics, and computers.

Christopher, Nick. *The Industrial Revolution, Migration, and Immigration*. New York, NY: PowerKids Press, 2016.
This book explores the effects the Age of Industrialization had on issues such as immigration and migration to the United States.

Gray, Leon. *Horrible Jobs of the Industrial Revolution*. Oxford, UK: Oxford Raintree, 2016.
Despite improvements to many aspects of life, the Industrial Revolution also introduced negative changes, including the jobs detailed by this book.

Jensen, Oliver. *The American Heritage History of Railroads in America*. New York, NY: Bonanza, 1981.
This illustrated volume traces the origins and development of American railroads, which were a critical component of the Industrial Revolution.

Wolfe, James, and Christine Poolos. *The Industrial Revolution: Steam and Steel*. New York, NY: Britannica Educational Publishing, 2016.
This detailed text explains the important and complex ways that the Industrial Revolution impacted the economy of the world.

Websites

Economic Growth and the Early Industrial Revolution (www.ushistory.org/us/22a.asp)
This website has an overview of some of the earliest causes and effects of the Industrial Revolution in America, as well as links to further information.

History Times: The Industrial Revolution (www.gilderlehrman.org/history-by-era/gilded-age/essays/history-times-industrial-revolution)
This website offers in-depth explanations behind many of the important dates and events of the Industrial Revolution, as well as a detailed library for further reading.

Industrial Revolution (www.history.com/topics/industrial-revolution).
Hosted by the History Channel, this website has detailed information as well as links to multimedia coverage of the Industrial Revolution.

Railroads Archive (www.newberry.org/railroad-archives)
This website, hosted by the Newberry Library, contains a wealth of information, including primary source documents, about railroad history in America.

"Why the Industrial Revolution Didn't Happen in China" (www.washingtonpost.com/news/wonk/wp/2016/10/28/why-the-industrial-revolution-didnt-happen-in-china/?utm_term=.aef035027346)
This article explores social, cultural, and economic forces that caused the Industrial Revolution to take hold in America instead of China.

Index

Picture Credits

Cover, pp. 21, 39 Print Collector/Contributor/Hulton Archive/Getty Images; pp. 4-5 NYPL NYPL/Science Source/Getty Images; pp. 6 (top left), 48 Stock Montage/Contributor/Archive Photos/Getty Images; pp. 6 (top and bottom right), 18, 23, 33 Courtesy of the Library of Congress; pp. 6 (bottom left), 16, 71 Hulton Archive/Stringer/Hulton Archive/Getty Images; p. 7 (top) Wirtz Library/Wikimedia Commons; pp. 7 (bottom), 35, 47, 57, 61, 66, 78, 79 Bettmann/Contributor/Bettmann/Getty Images; pp. 9, 45 Hulton Archive/Stringer/Archive Photos/Getty Images; pp. 11, 28, 31, 51, 89 Universal History Archive/Contributor/Universal Images Group/Getty Images; pp. 14, 32, 54 UniversalImagesGroup/Contributor/Universal Images Group/Getty Images; p. 26 Chris Hunter/Contributor/Corbis Historical/Getty Images; p. 37 Interim Archives/Contributor/Archive Photos/Getty Images; pp. 42–43 Buyenlarge/Contributor/Archive Photos/Getty Images; p. 59 Frank Scherschel/Contrubitor/The LIFE Picture Collection/Getty Images; p. 64 American Stock Archive/Contributor/Archive Photos/Getty Images; p. 68 Sports Studio Photos/Contributor/Getty Images Sport/Getty Images; p. 73 PhotoQuest/Contributor/Archive Photos/Getty Images; p. 76 Hulton Deutsch/Contributor/Corbis Historical/Getty Images; p. 83 Science & Society Picture Library/Contributor/SSPL/Getty Images; p. 92 The Washington Post/Contributor/The Washington Post/Getty Images.

About the Author

Emily Mahoney is the author and editor of over a dozen nonfiction books for young readers on various topics. She has a master's degree in literacy from the University at Buffalo and a bachelor's degree from Canisius College in Adolescent Education and English. She currently teaches reading to middle school students and loves watching her students learn how to become better readers and writers. She enjoys reading, Pilates, yoga, and spending time with family and friends. She lives with her husband in Buffalo, New York, where she was born and raised.